FOR JEFFRESS,
EAT YOUR VEGGIES
&
BUON APPETITO!

Susan Spicer

contorni

by **Susan Simon**
Photographs by
Manfredi Bellati and
Quentin Bacon

Authentic Italian Side Dishes for All Seasons

contorni

CHRONICLE BOOKS
SAN FRANCISCO

Library of Congress Cataloging-in-Publication Data:

Simon, Susan,
   Contorni : authentic Italian side dishes for all seasons / by Susan Simon ;
photographs by Manfredi Bellati and Quentin Bacon.
      p. cm.
Includes index.
   ISBN 0-8118-3676-2
   1. Cookery (Vegetables) 2. Side dishes (Cookery) 3. Cookery, Italian. I. Title.
   TX801 .S5718 2003
   641.6'5—dc21

                          2002010087

Manufactured in China.

Prop and food styling by Darienne Sutton
Designed by Benjamin Shaykin
Composition by Kristen Wurz
Typeset in Hightower, Nobel, and Bodoni Egyptian

Front cover photograph by Quentin Bacon
Back cover recipe photographs by Quentin Bacon
Back cover location photographs by Manfredi Bellati

Distributed in Canada by Raincoast Books
9050 Shaughnessy Street
Vancouver, BC V6P 6E5

10 9 8 7 6 5 4 3 2 1

Chronicle Books LLC
85 Second Street
San Francisco, California 94105

www.chroniclebooks.com

Per Nally
Perche' . . .

contents

Una Storia d'Amore a 230 gradi C.

A Love Story at 450°F.

Once upon a time in SIDE DISH ALLEY *there was a great big* MESS. *Miss* MEDLEY *filled the* LETTUCE BAR *with gluttonous screams and spicy pleas because she still couldn't get it through her* PUMPKIN *head, by now* FRIED *from the heat of the situation, that she had waded through* THICK WHITE SAUCE, *only to find how wrong she had been to believe that* BRUSSELS SPROUT, *that Mr. R.T. Choke, who had said he would love her forever, hot and at room temperature, in* SWEET AND IN SOUR, *until grill do them part. "What was I thinking? I'm not really a big cheese, I'll* MO[U]LD *and I'll* MARINATE *while waiting for that unfaithful* POTATO *head." To lift her spirits, she dug deep into her pockets, found some* GOLD COINS, *and ordered a large flask of wine.*

—Sofia Taliani, *inspired by the recipes of* Contorni . . .

C'era una volta in via **Contorni** un gran **pasticcio**. La Signorina **Frittella** riempiva il Bar **Lattuga** di urla golose, parole piccanti. Non riusciva a mettersi nella **zucca** ormai fritta da quanto scottava, che era stata cosi **besciamella** da credere a quel **cavolino di Bruxelles,** a quel caro Signor **Ciofo**, che l'avrebbe amata per sempre nel bene e nel male, nel **agro** e nel **dolce**, in **padella**, alla **brace**. Che **cavolo** stavo pensando? Sono proprio una **mozzarella**! Sto fresca se aspetto quella **patata** infedele. Per tirarsi su il morale, si prese delle **monete d'oro** dale tasche e si ordino una fiaschetta di vino!

—Sofia Taliani, ispirato dalle ricette di *Contorni* . . .

introduction

The literal translation of the Italian *contorno* is "outline," "border," from the verb *contornare*, "to surround." A *contorno* is also a side dish served with *il secondo*, the main dish of the meal. Think of an outline as something that defines that which it borders. This is definitely the case with the *contorno*.

While the *contorno* as we know it today is a relatively new culinary concept, dating back only two hundred or three hundred years, it's an important addition to the Italian table. It balances a meal that was once completely lopsided. While the rich and powerful existed on meat—a real symbol of potence—the poor survived on vegetables, legumes, and grains. The *contorno* has another less nutritious, but equally important role in the Italian meal, or any meal for that matter: the variety and quantity of side dishes presented at table become a reason to socialize, a way of making conversation. Offer people a *contorno*, then ask them how they like the particular preparation style. A world of ideas opens.

The Greeks who colonized Italy were probably the first "cooks" to combine the plants and herbs they discovered growing in abundance on the land that they occupied. These combinations were the basis for what we now call salads. With the evolution of civilization, these salad greens were simply cooked and served as an afterthought with the overwhelmingly meat and fish meals of the rich. During the

Middle Ages, vegetables were, for all intents and purposes, eliminated from the diets of the wealthy population. (Maybe that was the problem!)

With the Age of Enlightenment came the return to variety at the table. However, a cooked vegetable, legume, or grain was a simple, straightforward, and frankly boring addition. Salads were the creative offerings. Raw combinations of leaves, herbs, fruits, and nuts made into elaborate towers graced the tables of the rich. The poor, who in my opinion have always shown us the way to solve problems—out of necessity—began to flavor their vegetables with bits of meat and preserved fish, to cook their grains with milk, and to add herbs to legumes.

As history continued to evolve, so did the food that fueled the civilization. The schism between the classes narrowed and differences in dining habits became less evident. The fourteenth-century wedding dinner of Violante Visconti and Lionel Plantagenet featured gold-leaf-covered entrées, a presentation the poor were able to mimic by coating their meats in bread crumbs and then cooking them in lard or oil.

While the original occupiers of the Italian peninsula, the Greeks, made salads, other invaders introduced their own foodstuffs and particular preparations to the cuisine of their adopted land. The Arabs not only brought citrus fruits and rice to Italy, but they also shared their predilection for sweet-and-sour foods, a perfect fit for the southern Italian palate. The French left the white sauce, called béchamel, which figures in many northern *contorni*.

The Jews, confined to the ghettos of the great cities of Venice and Rome, and bound by the dietary laws of their religion, became real, creative contributors to *la cucina italiana*. According to Giuseppe Maffioli, in his wonderfully informative *La cucina veneziana* (Franco Muzzio editore, 1982), the Jews imported plants and comestibles that the Venetian population had never seen. Such introductions prompted Pellegrino Artusi, author of the first "modern" Italian cookbook, *Culinary Science and the Art of Eating Well*, in 1891, to refer to eggplant and fennel as being "once considered the vile food of the Jews." Because biblical law prohibited the mixing of meat and dairy, the Jews invented dishes that combined cheese, butter, and/or milk with vegetables. Maffioli goes on to say that the Jews were extremely inventive cooks who ate in a more interesting and varied way than the rest of the population. Jewish cooking had other advantages, too, including economy and healthfulness.

Finally, the northeastern part of Italy, the area known as the South Tyrol, was once a part of the Austro-Hungarian Empire. After World War I, it was annexed to Italy, bringing along the cuisine of Mittel-Europa, which has integrated itself into *la cucina italiana* as well.

THIS COUNTRY, WHICH YOU PROBABLY WOULDN'T IMMEDIATELY THINK OF as a land of immigrants, is, in fact, a melting pot like our own. The invaders and occupiers of the Italian peninsula with their native cuisines were influential in the development of a pan-ethnic Italian way of cooking—which of course meant newer and more flavorful *contorni*.

The many contributions, the abundance of produce—Italy is a volcanic-soil-rich country where every nook and cranny, every creek and crevice are cultivated—and the evolution of a national dining style led to the creation of real *contorni*, interesting dishes that gave emphasis to the now-diminishing-in-importance main course of meat or fish. These were dishes that deserved the name *contorno*, that did outline, highlight, and border that which they accompanied.

Before I begin to describe the few "master" methods for cooking *contorni*, let me state for the record, for the thousandth time: FOLLOW THE SEASONS. Nothing is sadder than trying to make a tasty *parmigianina di melanzane* (eggplant parmesan) in the middle of the winter with bitter, tasteless eggplant. Buy, and use, what's in season. There's plenty of choice.

One time in Italy, while having my nails polished, I engaged the young manicurist in a time-honored discussion of favorite foods. It was she who stated with emphasis the importance of eating vegetables—all food—in their proper season, "... *se no, ti fa male lo stomaco*" (if you don't eat things in season, you'll get a stomachache). Words of wisdom.

Almost every vegetable in the universe can be **gratinato**, "gratinéed." The harder, denser vegetables, like celery root, potatoes, squashes, or even asparagus, usually are gratinéed, that is, baked and browned until golden, with the rich, white sauce, béchamel, and sometimes cheese. A lighter, more delicate vegetable like leeks might be gratinéed with shredded cheese, bread crumbs, and lots of butter. Sweet bell peppers are gratinéed with savory additions like anchovies, capers, olives, and bread crumbs.

Vegetables can be **affogata**, "drowned," a simple preparation in which the vegetable is first simmered in fragrant olive oil and water, then sautéed to a full, intense flavor. Greens and root vegetables are the most successfully drowned vegetables.

Sformate di verdure, "molded vegetable puddings," are popular, show-offy ways of making a *contorno* a special-occasion side dish. I've seen recipes for *sformate* from asparagus to artichokes, from carrots to cardoons. A less formal rendition of the *sformato* would be a *pasticcio*, literally "pie," although often it means a "mess." Indeed, it is a mess of savory ingredients, starring a vegetable, put together and baked.

Vegetables can be dipped in a **pastella**, a light batter, and deep-fried. They can be simply *saltate*, "sautéed." They can be pureed, although with less butter and cream than we use, or they can be *stufate*, "stewed," and *brasate*, "braised." With the addition of ingredients like raisins, olives, capers, anchovies, almonds, pine nuts, and fresh herbs, a plain preparation becomes more elaborate in a manner of minutes.

Some vegetable preparations have been co-opted from meat, fish, and game dishes. You can cook artichokes **alla cacciatora**, in a spicy tomato sauce, just as you do when you make the classic chicken cacciatore. You can make the recipe for

lemony green beans **in fricassea**, well, just like you do for chicken fricassee. Some other meat-named vegetable recipes can be downright puzzling to the cook, however. For example, *fagioli* **all'uccelletto**, a traditional recipe for *cannellini* (dried white beans), is named for the style in which little birds are prepared. *Funghi* **trippati**, stewed mushrooms, are cooked like the famous *trippa in umido*, stewed tripe. *Zucchine* **in carpione** are zucchini cooked like freshwater carp. Because this custom is accepted without a second thought, dishes that are personal creations are given animal-referenced names. You'll find a recipe from my friend Antonia Jannone that she calls **topi morti**, "dead mice." Nothing, of course, could be further from dead mice than these eggplant-stuffed roasted peppers. It's just how they appear when they're all lined up in a baking dish.

Fresh vegetables are not the only ingredients used for making interesting *contorni*. Dry ingredients, perfect for keeping on your pantry shelves, are ideal when an emergency occurs—or just because polenta is such a fine side dish with a winy-rich beef stew. In addition to cornmeal; dried and canned beans; grains like rice, *farro*, barley, and millet; *pelati* (tinned, peeled tomatoes); anchovies; olives; and capers are good, basic items to have on hand. Besides polenta, a good risotto is a wonderful accompaniment to stewed or braised meats. Think about keeping a few pounds of good rice, like *carnaroli* or *vialone nano*, for making a risotto when guests appear unexpectedly.

Space is often an issue when putting together a cookbook. And never has that been more evident than when I was planning this one. What do I include? And what can be excluded with impunity? It's a tough call.

I didn't give you a recipe for batter-fried vegetables, but there are fried items in the book, with none more emblematic of Italian melting-pot food than *carciofi alla giudia*, Jewish-style deep-fried artichokes. This doesn't diminish the importance of *pastella*-covered fried artichokes. Let's just call the decision Susan's Choice. I didn't give you a recipe for *spinaci saltati*, "sautéed spinach," even though I love and always order it when in Italy. It's delicious, but so is the recipe that I have included,

Spinaci con Passi e Pinoli (page 35), spinach with raisins and pine nuts. It's sautéed spinach with a twist.

I went back and forth about twenty-five times on whether to include recipes for cardoons and *scorzanero*. Both are much-used sources for vegetable *contorni* in Italy. Even though cardoons and *scorzanero* are starting to show up more and more in American markets, I thought it best not to sacrifice a recipe for a more readily available ingredient for one that is, for now, a bit exotic. But I do have the room here to tell you a little something about cardoons and *scorzanero*.

The cardoon is, like the artichoke, a member of the thistle family. The plant is gigantic, and its stalks are used for food. (My sister, Laura, grows cardoons in her Nantucket garden for the Brobdingnagian, purple blossom alone.) When the plant reaches maturity, the stalks are folded, tied, and covered, to "blanch," or whiten, them. In other words, this is a "pain in the neck" operation, and it is no wonder Americans haven't enthusiastically embraced its cultivation. I digress. When you bring the celerylike stalks home from the market, they should first be peeled and parboiled before almost any cooking style you have planned. Cardoons, with their delicate, artichokelike flavor and celery texture are incredible when covered in a delicate *pastella* and deep-fried. They also can be made *agrodolce*, like *Peperoni Mandorlati* (page 50), *gratinati*, like the *Sedano-Rapa alla Besciamella* (page 125), or *affogati*. And so on.

Scorzanero is known as black salsify in English. A root vegetable, it looks like a slender, black parsnip, and tastes something like one, too. It can be made in *fricassea*, like the *fagiolini*, or *alla panna*, like the *topinambur*. Or it can be *affogato*, just like the *rape*.

I didn't include a recipe for *farro*, *orzo*, or *miglio* (spelt, barley, or millet) either even though many of my Italian friends use these grains for *contorni*. Cook the grains and then finish them like the *Ceci all'Arrabbiata* (page 43). Or cook the grains, then add butter and grated cheese like for the *Polenta Morbida* (page 77) for a perfectly delicious side dish.

I have one very obvious ingredient omission, and that's the ubiquitous broccoli rabe. It is served as a side dish in nearly every Italian restaurant in America. The book, however, has plenty of recipes that work beautifully with broccoli rabe. Try braising broccoli rabe like *Indivia Belga Brasata* (page 38) or quickly cooking it like *Broccoli alla Romana* (page 95).

You'll note certain ingredient preferences that I've requested for the recipes. When potatoes are involved, I nearly always ask for the excellently flavored Yukon gold. They most closely resemble the yellow-fleshed, all-purpose potato that you find in Italy, and their medium-starch texture is ideal for multiple applications. Flat-leaf parsley is a given—no substitutes accepted. It's the only parsley that has flavor. The inclusion of butter, milk, or cream usually signals that the recipe has its provenance in northern Italy. Please, don't try to use nonfat dairy products in place of whole-milk ones. The flavor shouldn't be compromised. Just eat a little less! A recipe that starts with something being sautéed in olive oil will tell you that recipe comes from the center to the southern part of the country, where olive oil is produced. I use pure olive oil, often labeled simply olive oil, for cooking, and extra-virgin oil for finishing, when I want a more emphatic taste.

Mi auguro that you'll enjoy the recipes, that they will inspire you to leave the confines of the instructions and be creative with the fresh, in-season ingredients that you find on the produce shelves of your local supermarket, at a farm stand, or in your very own garden. *Mi auguro anche*—"it's also my wish"—that with these recipes you will begin to think about the side dish as a surrounding, a border or outline that gives emphasis to the main dish. It should never be an afterthought, something that you add because you believe that you must. In other words, think about *un contorno* as a graceful accompaniment.

Buon Appetito.

primavera *spring*

I

serves 6 Whomever you ask in Italy for a recipe for *carciofi alla romana* will undoubtedly give you this one. It's enduring, unalterable. As a matter of fact, if you were to ask an Italian for an artichoke recipe, *qualsiasi,* "anyone," the response would be this one nine times out of ten. This never-changing method uses *mamelle,* artichokes that are, as luck would have it, similar to the globe artichokes grown in California and easily found in the produce department of most American supermarkets. ✳ There's a caveat when looking for artichokes for this recipe: search out those with a stem, as its inclusion is essential. ✳ Serve the artichokes hot or at room temperature with baked ham or roasted leg of lamb for a festive springtime meal.

carciofi alla romana
roman-style artichokes

2 lemons

6 globe artichokes with stems

3 cloves garlic, each sliced into 2 or 3 pieces

1 dried hot pepper such as cayenne, smashed

½ cup olive oil

2 cups water

1 teaspoon salt

1 tablespoon coarsely chopped fresh flat-leaf parsley

1. Prepare the artichokes: Cut 1 lemon in half. Squeeze both halves into a large bowl filled with water. Working with 1 artichoke at a time, and conserving its stem, remove the outside leaves by bending them backward and pulling down; they'll snap at the "meaty" point of the leaf. Pull away the leaves until you see only pale green ones, at about the halfway point of the artichoke. Use a very sharp knife to cut away the remaining leaf tops. Carefully peel the stem. Cut the artichoke in half lengthwise. Cut out the fuzzy choke. Immediately add the halves to the lemon water to prevent them from turning brown. Continue this process until all the artichokes have been prepared.

2. In a large skillet or sauté pan over medium heat, sauté the garlic and hot pepper in the olive oil until the garlic is golden, about 1 minute. Drain the artichokes, then lower the heat and add them, cut sides down, to the pan. Be careful, as the oil will splash when the wet artichokes hit the pan. Add the water, the juice of the remaining lemon, and the salt. Simmer uncovered, turning the artichokes occasionally. The artichokes are cooked when a tester easily passes through them, 30 to 45 minutes.

3. Remove from the heat and remove and discard the garlic and hot pepper. Stir in the parsley. Transfer the artichokes to a serving platter, then pour any liquid remaining in the pan over the top. Serve hot or at room temperature.

serves 6 to 8 *Alla cacciatora* is one of the many styles of food preparation usually associated with meat, but perfectly adaptable to vegetables. In this case, the garlicky, sweet tomato sauce works magic on the sometimes bitter artichokes. ※ The artichokes that we get here, in America, tend to be a little more bitter that the Italian ones, so here's a hint. The acidulated water used to keep the artichokes from turning black also helps to extract some of their bitter flavor. If you sense that your artichokes are unusually strong flavored, leave them in the lemon water for at least 30 minutes and up to an hour. ※ Serve the *carciofi* with meat loaf.

carciofi alla cacciatora
hunter-style artichokes

6 large artichokes

1 lemon

4 cloves garlic, smashed, then peeled

¼ cup olive oil

1 tin (1 pound) *pelati* (Italian peeled plum tomatoes), coarsely chopped, liquid reserved

½ cup water

1 teaspoon salt

1½ teaspoons dried oregano

½ teaspoon hot pepper flakes

1 tablespoon coarsely chopped fresh flat-leaf parsley

1. Prepare the artichokes as in step 1 in *Carciofi alla Romana* (page 23), using the lemon for the acidulated water. Cut each artichoke half in half again and return to the acidulated water.

2. In a large skillet or sauté pan over medium heat, sauté the garlic in the olive oil for 2 minutes to flavor the oil. Drain the artichokes, add them to the pan, and stir to coat them with the oil. Cook for 5 minutes. Add the tomatoes and their liquid, water, salt, oregano, and hot pepper flakes. Lower the heat, cover, and simmer until the artichokes are tender, 30 to 45 minutes. If the pan begins to dry out, add more water, ¼ cup at a time.

3. Remove from the heat and stir in the parsley. Transfer the artichokes to a serving platter and pour any liquid remaining in the pan over the top. Serve hot or at room temperature.

serves 6 I think that this single *contorno* inspired me to write this book. I tasted *frittella* for the first time, in the early spring, in Sicily, when I was a guest at the agricultural estate of the Tasca d'Almerita family, Regaleali. In addition to the world-class wines that the estate produces, the land grows the food that supplies the large family and the cooking school founded by the Marchesa Anna Tasca Lanza. ※ One day, Anna served *frittella*, made with the stars of the springtime harvest—artichokes, fava beans, and peas—at a casual luncheon. The flavor and texture of the dish were instantly pleasurable. Very green, slightly farinaceous, sweet, sour, and salty—all the sensations that give infinite satisfaction to the tongue. That day the *frittella* was served at room temperature with olive oil–preserved Sicilian tuna, a salad with tangerines, and a selection of cheeses. ※ *Frittella* is festive enough, and correct enough, to serve with an Easter or a Passover dinner.

frittella
spring vegetable medley

2 artichokes, about 1½ pounds total weight

1 lemon

1½ cups shelled fava beans (about 2½ pounds in their pods)

1 onion, coarsely chopped

¼ cup olive oil

¾ pound peas, shelled, or 1 cup frozen petite pois

1 cup water

1 teaspoon salt

½ teaspoon freshly ground white pepper

2 tablespoons white wine vinegar

1 tablespoon sugar

1. Prepare the artichokes as in step 1 in *Carciofi alla Romana* (page 23), using the lemon for the acidulated water. Thinly slice each artichoke half lengthwise. Return the pieces to the acidulated water.

2. In a large pot of boiling water, cook the fava beans for 2 minutes. Immediately plunge them into ice water to halt the cooking. Slip the skin off each bean.

3. In a large skillet or sauté pan over medium heat, sauté the onion in the olive oil until translucent, about 3 minutes. Add the fava beans and cook for 5 minutes. Drain the artichokes and add to the pan. Stir to combine and cook for 5 minutes. Add the peas, water, salt, and pepper. Cover and cook, stirring occasionally, until all the vegetables are tender, 15 to 20 minutes.

4. Add the vinegar and sugar, and stir to dissolve the sugar. Remove from the heat and serve hot or at room temperature.

serves 4 to 6 These deep-fried, whole artichokes, which come straight out of the Roman ghetto, are a reminder of the importance of vegetables on the Italian Jewish table, and of the Italian Jewish kitchen's gift to *la cucina italiana* as a whole. (Here's an opportunity for me to recommend that you read my introduction, where I have the space to talk about this influence in more detail.) ✳ Most of the recipes that I've read for making artichokes in this style talk about the difficulty involved when you try to open the leaves of the fried artichoke to create a chrysanthemumlike flower. Follow my directions and you will always achieve a beautiful blossom. Sometimes it will look like a chrysanthemum, other times, a golden thistle, a most appropriate likeness when you remember that the artichoke is indeed a giant thistle.

carciofi alla giudia
fried artichokes, jewish style

1 lemon

6 globe artichokes, or 12 baby artichokes

3 cups corn oil or as needed to fill the skillet or saucepan 5 inches deep

Salt and freshly ground black pepper

1 cup olive oil

1. Prepare the artichokes: Cut the lemon in half. Squeeze both halves into a large bowl filled with water. Working with 1 artichoke at a time, and conserving its stem, remove the outside leaves by bending them backward and pulling down; they'll snap at the "meaty" point of the leaf. Pull away the leaves until you see only pale green ones, at about the halfway point of the artichoke. Use a very sharp paring knife to trim away the tough green parts of the leaves that have remained, so that all you see is pale green. Carefully peel the stem. Trim the prickly pointed tops. Immediately add to the acidulated water.

2. In a deep skillet or saucepan over medium heat, warm the corn oil. Remove the artichokes from the water, one at a time. Hold the stem and press the leaves against a folded tea towel. Turn the artichoke in a circular motion to open the leaves. Use your fingers to rub a mixture of salt and pepper into and between the leaves. Add 2 or 3 (depending on the size) artichokes to the hot oil at a time. Cook, using a wooden chopstick to move them around in the oil, until completely golden, about 10 minutes for the small artichokes and 15 to 20 minutes for the larger ones. Drain on paper towels.

3. Just before serving: Pour the olive oil into a cast-iron skillet and heat over medium heat. To test if the oil is ready, stand the wooden chopstick in it; the oil should immediately sizzle around it. Use tongs to hold each artichoke, flower side down, in the oil. In 2 to 3 minutes, the artichoke should open like a chrysanthemum—or rose—in full bloom, if, in fact, it hasn't already done so with the first frying. Drain on paper towels and serve hot.

NOTE: *My friend Chris Trilevas, who owns the restaurant Col Legno in New York City, makes the best* carciofi alla giudia *this side of the Mediterranean. He reheats his once-fried artichokes by placing them on a wood-burning grill. This way they not only open and are crunchy, but they also have a faintly smoky flavor.*

serves 6 While the delicately but distinctively flavored asparagus doesn't need, or want, much fuss, this rich and rather elaborate preparation seems just right. The somewhat innocuous béchamel that covers the spears is like a cozy wrap, while the mild, nutty Emmentaler is the ribbon that ties up the package. Serve this luxurious *contorno* with a simple poached or cooked-in-parchment fish.

asparagi gratinati
gratinéed asparagus

2½ pounds medium-thick asparagus

béchamel sauce:

2 tablespoons unsalted butter

2 tablespoons all-purpose flour

1½ cups whole milk

½ teaspoon salt

¼ teaspoon freshly ground white pepper

¼ cup grated Parmesan cheese

¼ pound Emmentaler cheese, shredded

1. Trim the tough bottoms from the asparagus and peel them to within 1 inch of the tips. In a large pot of abundant boiling water, cook the asparagus until al dente, about 8 minutes. Drain and let cool.

2. Make the béchamel: In a small, nonreactive saucepan over medium heat, melt the butter. Add the flour and cook, stirring continuously, for 3 minutes. Gradually pour in the milk while stirring continuously, then cook, stirring, for another 3 minutes. When the mixture is the consistency of pancake batter, add the salt, pepper, and Parmesan. Cook, stirring, until the cheese has melted and combined with the sauce, about 2 minutes. Remove from the heat.

3. Preheat an oven to 375°F. Cover the bottom of a gratin dish with a very thin layer of the béchamel. Line up half of the asparagus, with the flower ends in the same direction, on the béchamel. Use half of the remaining béchamel to cover the asparagus. Sprinkle with half of the Emmentaler. Make another layer with the remaining asparagus, the flower ends in the opposite direction. Cover with the remaining béchamel, and then the remaining Emmentaler.

4. Bake until the sides are bubbling and the top and sides are browned, 20 to 30 minutes. Serve immediately.

serves 8 Tarts like these are often served as a *contorno* to accompany room-temperature cured meats like ham, salami, *soppressata*, and so on. They are the *ideal* companion. ✳ I created this recipe specifically for this book. Its authenticity is in its method and the combination of ingredients. The tarts can be free-form, like these, or they can be baked in tart pans with removable sides. Imagine that each *crostata* is a little springtime garden.

crostate di verdure primaverili
spring vegetable tarts

pastry:

1½ cups all-purpose flour

¼ cup extra-virgin olive oil

2 eggs

1 teaspoon salt

filling:

1 pound spinach, thoroughly rinsed and tough stems removed

2 tablespoons olive oil

1 pound asparagus, tough bottoms removed, peeled to within 1 inch of the tips, and halved lengthwise

½ cup whole-milk ricotta cheese

1 tablespoon grated Parmesan cheese

1 teaspoon coarse sea salt

Fresh chives, cut into 2-inch lengths (optional)

1. Make the pastry: In a food processor, combine the flour, olive oil, eggs, and salt and process until a dough forms, less than 1 minute. Divide the dough in half, form each half into a disk, wrap separately in waxed paper or plastic wrap, and chill for at least 10 minutes.

2. Make the filling: In a large skillet or sauté pan over medium heat, cook the spinach in 1 tablespoon of the olive oil until it has just wilted, about 45 seconds. Remove with a slotted spoon. Add the remaining 1 tablespoon olive oil to the pan over medium heat. Add the asparagus and cook, stirring occasionally, until the asparagus has wilted and is slightly browned, about 10 minutes. Remove from the pan.

3. Preheat an oven to 375°F. Remove the pastry from the refrigerator and let come to room temperature, about 15 minutes. On a lightly floured, smooth surface, roll out one of the disks into a ¼-inch-thick circle. Use 2 metal spatulas to place it on one side of an 11½-by-17½-inch baking sheet. Use your thumb and forefinger to roll in and pinch the edge to create a little rim. Repeat with the remaining disk. Spread half of the ricotta on the bottom of each pastry. Spoon half of the spinach on each ricotta layer. Place half of the asparagus, in a decorative way, over each layer of spinach. Sprinkle half of the Parmesan and salt over the top of each tart.

4. Bake until the pastry is golden, about 30 minutes. Let cool on a rack just a bit, then cut each *crostata* into 4 wedges. Garnish with chives, if using, and serve immediately.

serves 6 I like to cook fresh spinach in the spring and again in the fall to coincide with the two seasonal spinach harvests. This rustic, molded spinach dish has a counterpart in the *Autunno* section of this book, *Sformato di Spinaci* (page 89). Both are delicious, and each has its particular charms. This preparation is probably a little easier to make, and it's good both hot and at room temperature. The fancier *sformato*, bound together with béchamel, must be eaten while it's hot. *Pasticcio*, which translates colloquially as "mess," can be eaten at room temperature.

pasticcio di spinaci
spinach "mess" (pie)

3 pounds spinach, thoroughly rinsed and tough stems removed

3 tablespoons unsalted butter

1 onion, finely chopped

½ teaspoon salt

½ teaspoon freshly ground black pepper

½ teaspoon freshly grated nutmeg

1 cup torn bits of the white part of dense Mediterranean-style bread

1 cup whole milk

2 eggs

⅓ cup grated Parmesan cheese

3 hard-cooked eggs, peeled

1. In a large, heavy-bottomed saucepan over medium heat, using the moisture that has remained from rinsing, add the spinach in batches until it has all wilted. If the leaves seem too dry, add ¼ cup water at a time as needed. Remove from the heat, drain, pressing out excess moisture, and let cool. Finely chop.

2. In a large skillet or sauté pan over medium heat, melt 2 tablespoons of the butter. Sauté the onion until translucent, about 3 minutes. Add the chopped spinach, salt, pepper, and nutmeg and stir to combine. Remove from the heat and pour into a large bowl. Let cool.

3. In a small bowl, soak the bread in the milk. Squeeze dry and crumble the bread into the spinach mixture. Lightly beat the raw eggs. Add to the spinach mixture with the Parmesan and fold together.

4. Preheat an oven to 350°F. Use the remaining 1 tablespoon butter to grease a 9-by-5-inch loaf pan. Spoon the spinach mixture into the pan. Drop the hard-cooked eggs into the mix, end to end, so that when the loaf is cut, a slice of egg will decorate each piece. Put the loaf pan in a baking pan and add hot water to the baking pan to reach halfway up the sides of the mold.

5. Bake until the spinach mixture starts to pull away from the sides of the pan and a tester inserted into the center comes out clean, 45 minutes to 1 hour. Remove from the oven and invert onto a platter. Serve hot or at room temperature, cut into slices.

serves 4 to 6 This method for cooking greens is classic southern Italian. You can cook chicory, broccoli rabe, chard, and so on in this same manner. Sometimes an anchovy is added to the ingredient list as well. You'll need to adjust the cooking time accordingly to the type of greens, however. ✳ Spinach cooked this way is the perfect accompaniment to breaded, sautéed meats and *piccata*-style (sautéed with lemon) meats.

spinaci con passi e pinoli
spinach with raisins and pine nuts

1 tablespoon unsalted butter

1 tablespoon olive oil

1 small onion, finely chopped

1 rounded tablespoon pine nuts

4 teaspoons raisins

3 pounds spinach, thoroughly rinsed and tough stems removed

½ teaspoon salt

⅛ teaspoon ground cayenne

1. In a large, heavy-bottomed skillet or sauté pan over medium heat, melt the butter in the oil. Sauté the onion until translucent, about 3 minutes. Add the pine nuts and raisins and stir to coat with the onion mixture.

2. Add the spinach, in batches, stirring to combine with the other ingredients. Add the next batch as soon as the preceding batch has wilted, usually in less than 30 seconds. Cook until the spinach is tender, 3 to 5 minutes. Stir in the salt and cayenne. Serve immediately.

each recipe serves 6 Here are two popular ways to prepare peas as a *contorno*. Search out the first, tender, small peas of the season for these recipes. Alternatively, frozen petite pois can be respectably substituted. ❋ In both of these recipes, don't be concerned if all of the liquid hasn't been completely absorbed when the peas have finished cooking. These dishes are usually slightly wet—all the more reason to have pureed potatoes as a second *contorno* on the same plate. Serve either preparation with roast leg of lamb.

due con piselli
two with peas

piselli alla francese / french-style peas

2 tablespoons unsalted butter

6 scallions, white part only, coarsely chopped

1 small head Boston lettuce, leaves rinsed and chiffon-aded

3 fresh flat-leaf parsley sprigs

3 cups shelled peas (1³⁄₄ to 2 pounds in their pods)

³⁄₄ cup water

¹⁄₂ teaspoon salt

¹⁄₄ teaspoon freshly ground black pepper

1. In a saucepan over medium heat, melt the butter. Sauté the scallions until just translucent, about 2 minutes. Add the lettuce, parsley, and peas and stir to coat with the butter. Pour in the water, lower the heat, and simmer until the peas are tender, 10 (for frozen peas) to 30 (for fresh peas) minutes.

2. Season with the salt and pepper and serve immediately.

piselli con prosciutto / **peas with ham**

2 tablespoons unsalted butter

**2 scallions, white part only, or
1 spring onion, coarsely
chopped**

**3 cups shelled peas (1 ³/₄ to
2 pounds in their pods)**

³/₄ cup water

¹/₄ teaspoon salt

**¹/₄ teaspoon freshly ground
black pepper**

**¹/₄ pound boiled or baked
ham, cut into narrow strips**

1. In a saucepan over medium heat, melt the butter. Sauté the scallions until just translucent, about 2 minutes. Add the peas and stir to coat with the butter. Add the water, lower the heat, and simmer for 10 minutes.

2. Add the salt, pepper, and ham, mix well, and continue to simmer until the peas are tender, 5 (for frozen peas) to 20 (for fresh peas) minutes. Serve immediately.

serves 6 I always associate endive with springtime, even though it's available year-round in the produce section of most supermarkets. ✳ With this recipe, you have an example of the Italian inclination for cooking salad greens. You'll need to select a sturdy-leaved endive for this particular combination of ingredients and to use the braising technique. I've used Belgian endives here, but you can easily substitute the endive's botanical cousins, chicory or escarole. It's important only that your choice have a subtle bitter flavor, what the Italians call *amarognolo*. You must adjust the cooking time according to the green. In every case, the leaves need to remain slightly crisp. Serve with baked ham or pork roast.

indivia belga brasata
braised belgian endive

6 medium-large heads Belgian endive, about 2 pounds total weight

3 cloves garlic, smashed, then peeled

⅓ cup olive oil

¼ cup coarsely chopped, pitted black olives such as Gaeta or Kalamata

2 cups tomato puree

½ teaspoon salt

2 teaspoons dried oregano

1 tablespoon pine nuts

1. Remove and discard the tough, outer leaves from each endive, then cut in half lengthwise. Use a very sharp paring knife to cut out the core.

2. In a large skillet or sauté pan over medium heat, sauté the garlic in the olive oil for 2 minutes to flavor the oil. Add the halved endives and move them around the pan to thoroughly coat them with the oil. Add the olives, tomato puree, salt, and oregano and stir to combine. Lower the heat, cover, and cook, spooning the sauce over the endives every 10 minutes or so, until a tester easily passes through them, about 30 minutes.

3. Remove and discard the garlic. Transfer the endives to a serving dish, and sprinkle with the pine nuts. Serve immediately.

serves 4 to 6 Fricassee is not a cooking technique usually associated with vegetable preparation. But why not? Sautéing the main ingredient in butter, then adding it to a lemony sauce is what qualifies it as a fricassee. In other words, it's a *perfect* style for vegetables, especially tender green beans. ❊ Serve these beans hot for dinner with a roasted chicken, then offer any leftovers at room temperature with leftover chicken for lunch the next day.

fagiolini in fricassea
fricassee of green beans

1½ pounds green beans, vine end removed

1 tablespoon unsalted butter

1 tablespoon olive oil

1 teaspoon salt

¼ teaspoon freshly ground white pepper

2 egg yolks, lightly beaten

Juice of 1 lemon

1. In a large pot of abundant, salted boiling water, cook the green beans until tender, 12 to 15 minutes. Drain.

2. In a large skillet over medium heat, melt the butter in the olive oil. Add the green beans, salt, and pepper and stir to coat the beans with the butter and oil. Remove the skillet from the heat. Add the egg yolks and lemon juice and stir to completely coat the beans with the creamy lemon sauce.

3. Put the skillet back on low heat just for a few seconds, stirring continuously to ensure that the egg has cooked. Serve immediately or at room temperature.

serves 6 Molise is a relatively new (political) region of Italy, attaining its independence from the Abruzzi in 1963. Its traditions, however, are ancient. Located on Italy's east coast, Molise is rugged, mostly mountainous, with a short one-hundred-mile opening onto the Adriatic Sea. In spite of the terrain, vegetables and highly flavored herbs and spices grow happily in the region. Saffron comes from Molise. Olive oil from Molise is world renowned. Celery, particularly the widely used Pascal celery, has its roots in Italy (pun intended). ☀ This dish, attributed to Molise in Italian cookbooks, may be a traditional preparation—or simply a salute to an agriculturally rich region.

sedani alla molisana
celery in the style of molise

1 bunch celery

2 tablespoons plain dried bread crumbs

½ teaspoon salt

¼ teaspoon freshly ground white pepper

2 onions, coarsely chopped

2 tablespoons olive oil

½ cup water

8 black olives such as Gaeta or Kalamata, pitted and coarsely chopped

¼ teaspoon ground cloves

1. Remove and discard any torn or cracked outer celery ribs. Peel the remaining 10 or so outer ribs and cut crosswise into 4-inch pieces. Reserve the heart with the leaves. Parboil the celery pieces and the heart in salted boiling water for 5 minutes. Drain.

2. Arrange the celery pieces in a 7½-by-11-inch baking dish. Place the heart, fanned out, on top of the pieces. Sprinkle the bread crumbs, salt, and pepper evenly over the celery.

3. Preheat an oven to 350°F. In a skillet over medium heat, sauté the onions in the olive oil until translucent, about 3 minutes. Add the water and simmer just until it evaporates. Remove from the heat, stir in the olives, and then evenly distribute the mixture over the celery.

4. Shower the cloves evenly over the celery. Bake until the top is golden and the sides are bubbling, 30 to 40 minutes. Serve immediately.

serves 4 to 6 Talk about simple, talk about fast, and talk about tasty. Here it is: a no-fuss, quick, savory recipe that calls on products plucked from your pantry shelves. ☀ The tomato puree—*passata*—that may have been made from last summer's harvest is just the reminder you need that summer is on its way. ☀ Serve the chickpeas with grilled sausages or a hamburger.

ceci all'arrabbiata
"angry" chickpeas

2 cloves garlic, smashed, then peeled

1 small onion, coarsely chopped

½ teaspoon hot pepper flakes

2 tablespoons olive oil

3 cups dried chickpeas, cooked and drained, or 2 tins (19 ounces each) chickpeas, drained

1 cup tomato puree

1 teaspoon salt

2 tablespoons coarsely chopped fresh flat-leaf parsley

1. In a large skillet over medium heat, sauté the garlic, onion, and pepper flakes in the olive oil until the onion is translucent, about 3 minutes. Add the chickpeas, tomato puree, and salt and stir to combine. Lower the heat and simmer, uncovered, until the liquid is reduced by two-thirds, 15 to 20 minutes.

2. Remove from the heat and stir in the parsley. Serve hot or at room temperature.

serves 6 New York–based painter Linda Schrank celebrates her late-spring arrival at her Tuscan *casa colonica* (farmhouse) the same way each year. She gives a dinner party that honors her adopted second home, Italy. All the food from the first course to the dessert is red, white, and green, the colors of the Italian flag. Almost all of the ingredients come out of Linda's own *orto* (vegetable garden), lovingly tended year-round by a loyal gardener. ❋ With the table set under a grape-vine-covered pergola, guests sit down to a little bowl of green zucchini soup, white bread, and a little bowl of red gazpacho. The second course is *bresaola*, cured beef; *cannellini*, white beans from last year's harvest, cooked in the style of small birds—*all'uccelletto* (page 117); and these tender, young green beans with fresh herbs that come from the garden as well. Dessert is a scoop of lemon ricotta with raspberries and mint leaves. ❋ *Benvenuto in Italia.*

fagiolini del giardino della linda
linda's garden green beans

2 tablespoons extra-virgin olive oil

1 tablespoon fresh lemon juice

1 teaspoon red wine vinegar

½ teaspoon salt

¼ teaspoon freshly ground black pepper

1 tablespoon coarsely chopped fresh tarragon

1 teaspoon fresh thyme leaves

1½ pounds green beans, vine end removed

1. In a large serving bowl, whisk together the olive oil, lemon juice, vinegar, salt, and pepper until a tight emulsion is achieved. Stir in the fresh herbs. Set aside.

2. In a large pot of abundant boiling water, cook the green beans until tender but not mushy, about 8 minutes. Drain and immediately add to the serving bowl. Toss to completely coat with the dressing. Serve while still warm.

2
summer estate

In southern Italy, sweet peppers may tie or even surpass tomatoes as the most popular vegetable. They are also the vegetable of choice when a quick *contorno* is needed. In no time at all, they can be cut up and fried or sautéed. Add an anchovy or two, capers, olives, and fresh herbs in any combination or alone and you have the ideal partner for a grilled steak, roast chicken, or fried fish. ✳ But it's not just the southern Italians who appreciate the versatile pepper. The following recipes are a gastronomic minitour of Italy.

un quartetto di contorni con peperoni
a quartet of pepper side dishes

serves 8 It's difficult to call the kitchen of one region of Italy better than another. And I won't. I'll just report that those in the "know" (native Italians first and foremost) usually say that *la cucina emiliana*, the food of Emilia-Romagna, is Italy's most sophisticated cuisine. *Peperonata* seems to have Emiliana origins, although it's cooked all over the peninsula, give or take an ingredient.

peperonata / **sweet pepper stew**

1 cup thinly sliced onion

½ cup olive oil

½ teaspoon finely minced fresh hot pepper such as cayenne or Thai

9 bell peppers, in assorted colors, cut lengthwise into ½-inch-wide strips

1 pound plum tomatoes, peeled and coarsely chopped

1 tablespoon anchovy paste

Salt to taste

1. In a large, heavy-bottomed, nonreactive pot over medium heat, sauté the onion in the olive oil until translucent, about 3 minutes. Add the hot pepper, bell peppers, tomatoes, and anchovy paste. Stir to combine. Lower the heat a notch and simmer, cover askew, until the peppers are soft but not mushy, 30 to 40 minutes.

2. Remove from the heat and taste for salt. Let stand for a few minutes before serving. Serve warm or at room temperature. It will keep for up to a week refrigerated.

serves 6 *Bagna cauda,* "hot bath," is a traditional Piedmontese dish made with olive oil, butter, garlic, and anchovies. Typically all the ingredients for *bagna cauda* are added to a terra-cotta pot and cooked until the anchovies have melted and the garlic is soft. The pot is then placed on a small burner in the center of a table where the "bath" becomes a dip for raw vegetables. ❋ Peppers cooked *alla bagna cauda* take their cue from the traditional recipe by using the same ingredients but a slightly different method. The resulting flavor is extremely savory, making these peppers a sensational side dish for everything from a mixed-herb frittata to roast beef.

peperoni alla bagna cauda / sweet peppers, bagna cauda style

6 bell peppers, in assorted
   colors

Corn oil, if oven roasting

2 tablespoons unsalted butter

2 tablespoons olive oil

4 cloves garlic, thinly sliced

1 or 2 salt-packed anchovies,
   rinsed, filleted, and
   coarsely chopped, or
   3 oil-packed anchovy
   fillets, coarsely chopped

1. Roast the peppers over a gas flame until completely charred. Alternatively, preheat an oven to 450°F. Cut the peppers in half lengthwise, coat with a bit of corn oil, place, skin side down, on a baking sheet, and roast until charred, about 20 minutes.

2. Put the roasted peppers in a bowl and seal with plastic wrap. When cool enough to handle, after about 30 minutes, peel the skin from the peppers, then remove the stems, seeds, and membranes. Cut lengthwise into $^1/_2$-inch-wide strips. This can be done up to 8 hours before serving.

3. To serve, place the peppers in a shallow serving bowl. In a saucepan over low heat, melt the butter in the olive oil. Add the garlic and anchovies and cook until the garlic is soft but not golden and the anchovies have melted, 7 to 10 minutes. Pour over the peppers and serve immediately.

serves 8 I found a version of this recipe in a book called *La cucina dei buoni contorni* by Emilia Valli (Arnoldo Mondadori, 1988). While Signora Valli gives the reader little more than the ingredient list and the method, it would be my guess that the recipe is Sicilian—or at least Sicilian inspired. The ingredients tell me that. The Sicilians inherited the technique of sweet-and-sour flavoring from the Saracens (Arabs), who invaded the island in the first century and stayed on for three hundred years. Almonds grow profusely on Sicily and are used lavishly in the local kitchens. ❁ I'm fond of pairing this pepper dish with garlicky, grilled pork chops.

peperoni mandorlati / **sweet-and-sour peppers with almonds**

1 large onion, coarsely chopped

2 tablespoons olive oil

5 bell peppers, in assorted colors, cut lengthwise into ¼-inch-wide strips

1 pound plum tomatoes, peeled and coarsely chopped

¼ cup dried currants

1 teaspoon sugar

1 teaspoon salt

1 tablespoon red wine vinegar

2 tablespoons fresh lemon juice

¼ cup blanched almonds

1. In a large, heavy-bottomed, nonreactive skillet over medium heat, sauté the onion in the olive oil until translucent, about 3 minutes. Add the peppers and stir to combine with the onion. Add the tomatoes and lower the heat, then add the currants and stir to combine. Simmer for 8 minutes.

2. While the sauce is simmering: In a small bowl, stir together the sugar, salt, vinegar, and lemon juice until the sugar dissolves. Reserve.

3. In a small skillet over medium heat, toast the almonds until golden. Let cool and coarsely chop.

4. Remove the peppers from the heat and immediately add the vinegar mixture and the toasted almonds. Stir to combine and serve hot or at room temperature.

serves 6 For years, whenever I'm near a radio at noon, I tune in to "Food Talk," Arthur Schwartz's New York–based, nationally syndicated radio program. I have a great time listening to his food conversation, which touches on all sorts of interesting subjects from the latest trendy ingredient to where to dine near Yankee Stadium. ☀ However, it's Arthur's particular passion for Italian food, specifically the cuisine of Campania, the region that has Naples as its capital, that got me thinking that he might be willing to share a Neapolitan *contorno* recipe with me. After all, we were on "intimate" terms, his voice coming through a radio not two steps from me nearly every day. ☀ Arthur answered my request without hesitation when he forwarded this recipe for a highly flavored bell pepper gratin. It is from his book *Naples at Table* (HarperCollins, 1998).

peperoni gratinati / **gratinéed peppers**

6 large red bell peppers

1 or 2 salt-packed anchovies, rinsed, filleted, and finely chopped, or 3 oil-packed anchovy fillets, finely chopped

8 black olives such as Gaeta or Kalamata olives, pitted and coarsely chopped

1 rounded tablespoon salt-packed capers, rinsed and coarsely chopped

5 tablespoons extra-virgin olive oil

1 teaspoon dried oregano

2 tablespoons coarsely chopped fresh flat-leaf parsley

2 large cloves garlic, minced

½ cup plain dried bread crumbs

1. Roast, peel, and cut the peppers as for *Peperoni alla Bagna Cauda* (page 49).

2. In a shallow baking dish, about 2-quart capacity, combine the peppers, anchovies, olives, capers, olive oil, oregano, parsley, and garlic. Toss to thoroughly combine.

3. Preheat an oven to 400°F. Add all but 1 tablespoon of the bread crumbs to the mixture. Toss again and spread evenly in the dish. Sprinkle the remaining tablespoon of bread crumbs evenly over the top. Bake until the sides are bubbling, about 20 minutes.

4. Turn the oven to broil. Place the dish under the broiler until the top crumbs are lightly toasted, about 5 minutes. Serve warm or at room temperature.

serves 4 to 8 Here's another example of the Italian penchant for naming vegetable dishes for animals. In this case, it is *topi morti*, "dead mice," a classic Neapolitan preparation usually called *peperoni imbottiti*, or "stuffed peppers," but here given a strictly Jannone family pet [*sic*] name! ✳ Once you make this recipe and line up the chubby pepper bundles in a baking dish, you'll have to admit that the resemblance to somnolent mice (my take) is uncanny. ✳ Try to appreciate the humor, and its origins, and enjoy this truly tasty dish with any meat or fish that has lots of lemon flavoring.

topi morti
eggplant-stuffed peppers

4 red bell peppers

2 cloves garlic, smashed, then peeled, and each cut into 3 or 4 slices

1 fresh or dried hot red pepper such as cayenne or Thai

1 cup extra-virgin olive oil

2 eggplants, 2 ½ pounds total weight, cut into ½-inch dice

¼ cup coarsely chopped fresh basil

2 teaspoons salt

½ cup grated Parmesan or Romano cheese

1. Roast and peel the peppers as for *Peperoni alla Bagna Cauda* (page 49), and cut them in half lengthwise if they were roasted over a flame. Set aside.

2. In a large skillet or sauté pan over medium heat, sauté the garlic and hot pepper in the olive oil. When the garlic is pale gold, add the eggplant, in batches, stirring occasionally with a wooden spoon. When most of the sides of the eggplant pieces are browned, after about 3 or 4 minutes, lift them from the pan with a wire-mesh strainer. Use the wooden spoon to push all the excess oil back into the pan for the next batch. Be careful not to remove the hot pepper and garlic. Add the eggplant to a bowl.

3. Add any remaining pan oil, the basil, and the salt to the eggplant and stir to combine.

4. Preheat an oven to 350°F. Lay the roasted pepper halves, skinned sides down, on a flat surface. Mound one-eighth of the eggplant mixture in the center of each pepper half. Fold the pepper over the mixture to close. You'll have to squeeze it a bit, forming an egg shape. Place the filled peppers, seam sides down, in a baking dish. Sprinkle all the cheese evenly over the peppers.

5. Bake until the cheese has melted and the peppers closest to the sides of the dish are browned, 20 to 30 minutes. Serve immediately.

serves 4 to 8 During my trips to Italy, I'm always on the lookout for newly published cookbooks. I found one of the most charming books—ever—during an autumn sojourn to do some research for this book. Isabella Quarantotti De Filippo, wife of the late, renowned, and beloved writer, director, and actor Eduardo De Filippo, put together a collection of her husband's favorite recipes in a slim volume called *Si cucine cumme vogli'I* (*Cooking, My Way*). De Filippo, who felt most at home in the theater, also wrote and directed dozens of movies, among them *Yesterday, Today, and Tomorrow* with Marcello Mastroianni. Neapolitan through and through, De Filippo loved to serve the simple foods of his native city to friends and colleagues, a gesture he considered *una cosa sacra*, "a sacred thing." ☀ Here's *il maestro* De Filippo's version of a traditional Neapolitan dish. He reminds the reader that the *scarpone* were typically cooked in pizza ovens and are boiling hot when ready. *Attenzione.*

melanzane a scarpone
eggplant "shoes"

4 small eggplants, 6 to 8 inches long

1 pound very ripe tomatoes, peeled, seeded, and chopped

2 tablespoons coarsely chopped, pitted black olives such as Gaeta or Kalamata

¼ cup salt-packed capers, rinsed

½ cup extra-virgin olive oil

2 cloves garlic, each cut into 4 slices

1 teaspoon dried oregano

1 teaspoon coarse sea salt

1. Cut the vine end off each eggplant. Cut the eggplants in half lengthwise. Use a very sharp paring knife to make a deep—almost to the skin—crisscross grid on the flesh side of each half.

2. Put the tomatoes, olives, and capers in a bowl and toss together.

3. Preheat an oven to 450°F. Using 2 tablespoons of the olive oil, grease a rimmed baking sheet. Line up the eggplant halves, skin sides down, on the sheet. Insert a garlic slice into the center of each eggplant half. Spoon the tomato mixture over the eggplant. Drizzle the remaining 6 tablespoons olive oil over the eggplant. With the oregano between your fingers, shower it over the eggplant. Do the same with the salt.

4. Bake until the eggplant is soft and slightly collapsed, about 45 minutes. It will be red-hot; let cool a bit before serving, or serve at room temperature.

serves 6 to 8 Eggplant cutlets are sometimes called poor man's milanese, referring to the classic breaded and fried veal cutlet preparation *alla milanese*. In fact, historically, *cotoletta alla milanese* is itself a poor man's dish. In 1368, when Violante Visconti married Lionel Plantagenet in her hometown, Milan, everything on the elaborate wedding banquet, from whole suckling pigs to wild hare, from sturgeon to trout, was covered in gold leaf. ☀ *Cotoletta alla milanese* was born when the poorer inhabitants of the city wished to copy the golden food of the rich. The effect was achieved by coating their meat in bread crumbs, then frying it in oil. These eggplant cutlets, direct descendants of the Visconti wedding reception dinner, will elevate any summertime buffet offering.

melanzane a cotoletta, un po' piccanti
lightly spiced eggplant cutlets

**2 large eggplants, about
   2 pounds total weight**

Salt

1 cup all-purpose flour

½ teaspoon ground cayenne

2 teaspoons dried oregano

4 eggs

**1½ to 2 cups plain dried
   bread crumbs**

2 cups corn oil

1. Cut the ends off the eggplants. Peel them and cut crosswise into ¼-inch-thick slices. Layer the slices in a colander, salting every other layer. Cover the top layer with paper towels, and weight down with a heavy object such as a cast-iron skillet. Let drain for 30 minutes.

2. In a pie plate, stir together the flour, cayenne, and oregano until well mixed. In a shallow bowl, beat the eggs until blended. In another pie plate, spread the bread crumbs.

3. Pour the oil into a skillet or sauté pan and place over medium-low heat.

4. While the oil heats, rinse the eggplant slices and squeeze dry. One at a time, dust them with the flour, dip them in the eggs, and then thoroughly coat them with the bread crumbs, pressing firmly to ensure that the crumbs stick. Set aside on a platter.

5. To test if the oil is ready, stand a wooden spoon or chopstick in it; it should immediately sizzle around it. Fry the eggplant, 3 or 4 slices at a time, in the hot oil, turning them at least once. They need to have a deep golden crust and be soft on the inside, which will take at least 2 minutes' cooking time. If they turn dark too quickly, lower the heat. Drain on paper towels. Serve hot or at room temperature.

serves 6 This light eggplant *parmigianina* bears absolutely no resemblance to the breaded, fried, almost unidentifiable ingredient, shrouded in burn-the-roof-of-your mouth "red" sauce, then glued together with obscene amounts of rubbery mozzarella, that's often found in corner pizza parlors. I painted this unattractive picture on purpose as a way of urging you to try this preparation for eggplant Parmesan—the results will be epiphanic for you. You will be able to taste and identify every ingredient in this *contorno*. *Parmigianina di melanzane* gets its name not because it originated in Parma—it's a typically Neapolitan dish—but because of the Parmesan cheese that's used in its creation. ✳ Use small, fresh eggplants for this recipe and you won't have to salt and drain them first.

parmigianina di melanzane
eggplant parmesan

1 cup olive oil

4 or 5 small eggplants, about 2¹/₂ pounds total weight, ends trimmed and cut lengthwise into ¹/₄-inch-thick slices

2 cloves garlic, smashed, then peeled

2 small, fresh hot peppers such as Thai, smashed

1 tin (2 pounds) *pelati* (Italian peeled plum tomatoes), undrained, passed through a food mill or chopped

1 teaspoon salt

¹/₄ cup coarsely chopped fresh flat-leaf parsley

¹/₄ cup coarsely chopped fresh basil

1 cup grated Parmesan cheese

1 tablespoon unsalted butter, cut into bits

1. In a large skillet or sauté pan over medium heat, warm all but 1 tablespoon of the olive oil. Fry the eggplant, a few slices at a time, until golden, 1 to 2 minutes. Drain on paper towels.

2. In a saucepan over medium heat, warm together the remaining 1 tablespoon olive oil, the garlic, and the hot peppers to flavor the oil. When the garlic is pale gold, add the tomatoes and salt. Lower the heat and simmer for 10 minutes. Remove from the heat, remove and discard the garlic cloves, and stir in the parsley and basil.

3. Preheat an oven to 375°F. Cover the bottom of a large, shallow baking dish with some of the tomato sauce. Add a layer of eggplant slices, another layer of tomato sauce, and a generous sprinkle of the Parmesan. Continue layering until all the ingredients are used up, ending with Parmesan. Dot the top with butter.

4. Bake until the sides are bubbling and the cheese has melted and is slightly golden, 30 to 40 minutes. Allow to rest for a few minutes before serving.

serve 6 Squash blossoms are stuffed, fried, baked, stewed, and folded into pasta sauces and risottos all over Italy. This preparation is typical of what you'd find in stuffed, baked blossoms on a family table in San Remo or in Portofino, both towns in the Liguria region, jackknifed into the northwest coast of Italy. In fact, you'd more than likely find this same filling in many different vegetables in Liguria, an area famous for its stuffed vegetables. ☀ I specify squash blossoms, which show up in markets mid- to late summer and are a bit larger than zucchini blossoms. If you use zucchini blossoms, you may not need to cut them in half. ☀ This is an irresistible side dish with simple grilled fish.

fior di zucca al forno
baked squash blossoms

1 pound potatoes such as Yukon gold or Yellow Finn

½ cup (¼ pound) unsalted butter

½ cup whole milk

1 egg, lightly beaten

½ cup grated Parmesan cheese

1 clove garlic, minced

½ cup coarsely chopped fresh basil

1 teaspoon salt

12 squash blossoms or 24 zucchini blossoms

1. In a large pot of abundant boiling water, cook the potatoes in their jackets until a tester easily passes through them, about 20 minutes. Drain. Peel them as soon as they are cool enough to touch, then push them through a ricer or a food mill held over a bowl.

2. Reserve 2 teaspoons of the butter; melt the rest and add it to the bowl holding the potatoes along with the milk, egg, Parmesan, garlic, basil, and salt. Stir to combine.

3. Preheat an oven to 375°F. Use the remaining 2 teaspoons butter to grease an 11-by-17-inch baking dish. Cut each squash blossom in half lengthwise. Place a rounded tablespoon of the potato filling in the cavity of each blossom. Fold the petal over the opening and place, seam side down, in the prepared baking dish. If using zucchini blossoms, gently open the whole blossom and fill from the top. Continue until all the blossoms are filled.

4. Bake until the edges of the blossoms are golden and bubbles are visible along the sides of the dish, about 30 minutes. Serve immediately.

serves 6 to 8 The Italians love to scare vegetarians to death with provocative preparations for vegetables. This one for zucchini cooked like carp hasn't a scrap of offending ingredients. ✳ These fried, then marinated zucchini are full of complex flavor and are a perfect accompaniment to simple, roasted or grilled chicken. Because this dish can be refrigerated for up to three days, it's the perfect side dish to serve with a lunchtime sandwich or leftover roasted chicken.

zucchine in carpione
zucchini cooked like carp

½ cup all-purpose flour

2 pounds small to medium
    zucchini, ends trimmed
    and cut lengthwise into
    slices no more than
    ¼ inch thick

¾ cup corn oil

1 onion, cut into 6 wedges
    and each wedge stuck
    with 1 whole clove

3 cloves garlic, peeled but
    left whole

2 tablespoons olive oil

¾ cup white wine vinegar

½ cup dry white wine

½ cup water

8 fresh sage leaves

1 teaspoon salt

1. Spread the flour in a pie plate. Working in small batches, lightly flour the zucchini slices, pressing firmly to ensure that the coating adheres.

2. Pour the corn oil into a large skillet or sauté pan over medium heat and heat for 3 minutes. Fry the zucchini, 5 to 6 slices at a time, turning once, until pale gold, about 2 minutes on each side. Drain on paper towels, then place in a gratin dish or other baking dish.

3. In a skillet over medium heat, sauté the onion wedges and whole garlic cloves in the olive oil until the onion is translucent, about 5 minutes. Add the vinegar, wine, water, sage, and salt to the pan and simmer for 5 minutes to blend the flavors. Pour over the zucchini. You may have to adjust the zucchini to make sure that it is all immersed in the marinade. Let cool.

4. Cover the dish with plastic wrap and refrigerate for at least 12 hours before serving. The zucchini will keep for up to 3 days in the refrigerator.

serves 4 to 8 Stuffed zucchini are among the most familiar Italian food preparations. These *zucchine farcite*, on a bed of chopped fresh tomatoes, bear little resemblance to the fat-laden stuffed zucchini served at many Italian-American restaurants. ❋ The herby, light, and fresh taste of this summertime *contorno* makes it an ideal accompaniment to any meat or fish cooked on an outdoor grill.

zucchine farcite
stuffed zucchini

4 zucchini, about 1½ pounds total weight

1 onion

¼ cup olive oil

1¼ pounds plum tomatoes, peeled and diced

½ cup coarsely chopped fresh flat-leaf parsley

½ cup coarsely chopped fresh basil

¼ cup plain dried bread crumbs

½ cup grated pecorino romano or other hard, sharp cheese

2 eggs, lightly beaten

¼ teaspoon salt

¼ teaspoon freshly ground black pepper

1. Trim the ends, then cut the zucchini in half lengthwise. Scoop out the center of each zucchini half, leaving a ¼-inch-thick shell. Finely chop the pulp and the onion together.

2. In a skillet or sauté pan over medium heat, cook the zucchini-onion mix in 3 tablespoons of the olive oil for 2 or 3 minutes, stirring occasionally. Add half of the tomatoes, the parsley, and the basil. Lower the heat and cook, stirring occasionally, until the mixture is soft, about 15 minutes longer. Remove to a bowl and let cool.

3. Add the bread crumbs, cheese, eggs, salt, and pepper to the cooled zucchini mixture and stir to thoroughly combine.

4. Preheat an oven to 350°F. Use the remaining 1 tablespoon of oil to grease a baking dish. Evenly spread the remaining tomatoes on the bottom of the dish. Fill the zucchini halves with the cooled zucchini mixture. Place the halves on top of the diced tomatoes.

5. Bake until the bottom tomato layer is bubbling and the tops of the zucchini have formed a golden crust, 30 to 40 minutes. Serve immediately or at room temperature.

serves 4 to 6 If you hear *scapece* used to describe a recipe, for fish sometimes, and very often with vegetables, especially with zucchini and eggplant, it means that the main ingredient has been fried and then marinated. This method has led me and others to believe that the word *scapece* comes from the Spanish *escabeche,* a way of "cooking" raw fish by marinating it. ✳ You can make refrigerator *scapece* like this one, in which you marinate and then refrigerate the dish for consumption within four or five days. Or you can make preserved *scapece* by adding the vegetables to sterilized jars and then processing them in a water bath according to the manufacturer's directions. ✳ Knowing there's a bowl of zucchini *scapece* in the fridge, or in a jar on the shelf, to have as a last-minute—delicious—side dish for anything you're serving is indeed comforting.

zucchine in scapece
marinated zucchini

2½ pounds zucchini, ends trimmed and sliced on the diagonal to make ¼-inch-thick ovals

1 cup olive oil

2 cloves garlic, thinly sliced

2 tablespoons fresh mint leaves

1 tablespoon coarse sea salt

¼ cup red wine vinegar

1. In a large skillet or sauté pan over medium heat, fry the zucchini, in batches, in the olive oil. Use tongs to turn the zucchini to ensure that both sides are a deep gold, and plan on 2 or 3 minutes' total cooking time. Transfer the slices to a plate. In this case it's not necessary to drain the excess oil.

2. In a shallow glass or ceramic serving bowl, make layers with the zucchini, the garlic slices, the mint leaves, and a sprinkle of salt. Pour the vinegar over everything. Seal with plastic wrap and refrigerate for at least 4 hours and up to 5 days before serving.

makes about thirty-six 1½-inch croquettes I always think of *crocchette* as the ultimate *rosticceria* food. *Rosticcerie* are Italian take-out food shops that specialize in rotisseried chicken and accompaniments, which are invariably fried items. Good news for the *casalinga*, "housewife"—yummy food without the smoke and smell! ✳ But I love *crocchette*, and the last time I looked, a *rosticceria* still hadn't opened nearby. ✳ Make these Genoese-style croquettes in the morning before it gets too hot, then reheat them just as your chicken is coming off the grill. Pour yourself an icy glass of Bianco di Cinqueterre. Ah, *la vita e* indeed *bella*!

crocchette di patate alla genovese
potato croquettes in the style of genoa

1¾ pounds potatoes such as Yukon gold or Yellow Finn

4 tablespoons unsalted butter, at room temperature

½ cup grated Parmesan cheese

½ cup coarsely chopped fresh basil

1 tablespoon pine nuts

1 teaspoon salt

¼ teaspoon freshly ground black pepper

3 eggs, separated

1 cup plain dried bread crumbs

2 cups corn oil

1. In a large pot of abundant boiling water, cook the potatoes in their jackets until a tester easily passes through them, about 20 minutes. Drain. As soon as they are cool enough to touch, peel them, then push them through a ricer or food mill held over a large bowl.

2. Add the butter, Parmesan, basil, pine nuts, salt, and pepper to the potatoes and stir to combine. Add the egg yolks and again stir to combine.

3. In a shallow bowl, lightly beat the egg whites. Spread the bread crumbs in a pie plate. Form the potato mixture into egg-shaped croquettes about 1½ inches long, pressing gently but firmly to keep the shape. One at a time, coat the croquettes with the beaten egg whites, then roll them in the bread crumbs. Set aside on a platter.

4. Pour the oil into a skillet or sauté pan over medium heat and heat to 365°F. Add the croquettes, 4 or 5 at a time, to the hot oil. Move them around with a wooden spoon or a wooden chopstick until they're deep gold on all sides, 4 or 5 minutes. Drain on paper towels.

5. The croquettes may be kept warm in a 250°F oven until all are cooked and ready to serve. Or they may be made up to 8 hours ahead and reheated in a 400°F oven. Serve piping hot.

serves 6 to 8 My half-English, half-Italian friend Nally Bellati has lived more than half of her life in her mother's—and her husband's—native Italy. However, Nally still yearns for the comforting food of her English childhood. Thinking about a favorite English dessert, she was inspired to create a savory crumble in her Veneto kitchen that pays homage to the two countries of her heritage. ✳ Her clever *contorno* uses the glorious vegetables of summertime to make a tasty Mediterranean-style filling, and then tops it with a crunchy mix of ingredients that lets you know that while this dish may have its origins in an English kitchen, it has become *italianissimo!*

sbrisolona di verdure estive
summer vegetable crumble

3 cloves garlic, smashed, then peeled

1 dried hot pepper such as cayenne or Thai

1 cup olive oil

1³/₄ pounds eggplant, ends trimmed and cut into ¹/₂-inch dice

2 pounds zucchini, ends trimmed and cut into ¹/₂-inch dice

1 pint cherry tomatoes, stemmed

¹/₂ cup coarsely chopped fresh basil

³/₄ teaspoon salt

topping:

¹/₂ cup all-purpose flour

¹/₂ cup plain dried bread crumbs

2 tablespoons unsalted butter

¹/₄ cup grated Parmesan cheese

2 teaspoons black olive paste

1. In a large skillet or sauté pan over medium heat, sauté the garlic and hot pepper in the olive oil. When the garlic is pale gold, cook the diced eggplant, in batches, stirring occasionally with a wooden spoon. When most of the sides of the eggplant pieces are browned, after about 6 or 7 minutes, lift them from the pan with a wire-mesh strainer. Use the wooden spoon to push all the excess olive oil back into the pan for the next batch. Be careful not to remove the garlic and hot pepper. Add the eggplant to a bowl. When all the eggplant is cooked, brown the zucchini in the same way and add to the bowl.

2. Raise the heat to high and add the cherry tomatoes to the pan. Sauté them until they appear slightly blistered, about 2 minutes. Add to the bowl. Then, add the basil and salt to the bowl and stir to combine. Transfer the mixture to a baking dish.

3. Preheat an oven to 400°F. In another bowl, make the topping: Combine the flour, bread crumbs, butter, Parmesan, and olive paste. Use your fingers to rub the ingredients together until the mixture appears crumbly. Scatter the topping evenly over the vegetables.

4. Bake until the sides are bubbling and the topping has deepened in color, about 25 minutes. Serve immediately.

serves 4 to 8 Tomatoes and Italy are synonymous. Tomato sauce for pasta, pizza with tomatoes, *insalate con pomodori*—all are part of everyday meals *all'italiano*. In the summertime, you'll find lots of recipes for room-temperature stuffed tomatoes—with seafood, with rice salad, and so on. While a cooked stuffed tomato is not a rarity, it's usually more or less like this recipe. Simple, savory, and to the point. ※ These tomatoes are heavenly served beside a charcoal-grilled steak.

pomodori al forno
baked garlicky tomatoes

¼ cup plus 1 tablespoon olive oil

4 medium to large ripe tomatoes, stemmed and sliced in half horizontally

2 large cloves garlic, finely chopped

¾ cup plain dried bread crumbs

½ cup coarsely chopped fresh basil

½ cup coarsely chopped fresh flat-leaf parsley

1 teaspoon salt

2 tablespoons unsalted butter

8 anchovy fillets (optional)

1. In a large, heavy-bottomed, nonreactive skillet or sauté pan over medium-high heat, cook the ¼ cup olive oil for a minute or two before adding the tomatoes, cut sides down. (You may have to cook the tomatoes in 2 batches.) Let the tomatoes cook for 4 or 5 minutes. They should release some juice and be slightly browned on the sliced side. Place the cooked tomatoes, cut sides up, in a baking dish that has been greased with the remaining 1 tablespoon olive oil.

2. Lower the heat under the skillet to medium and sauté the garlic until golden. Add the bread crumbs and combine with the liquid in the pan. Turn off the heat and stir in the herbs and salt.

3. Preheat an oven to 450°F. Generously cover the top of each tomato with the bread crumb mixture. Divide the butter into 8 pieces and place on top of each of the tomatoes. You may want to place an anchovy fillet over each tomato as well.

4. Bake until the topping is golden and the tomatoes are bubbling and sizzling, about 15 minutes. Serve immediately or at room temperature up to 2 hours after baking.

autunno *fall*

3

serves 8 *Cianfotta, il contorno di tutti i contorni,* "the side dish of all side dishes," has its origins in Campania, the region just south of Rome. It is usually made in the summer with eggplant, peppers, onions, and potatoes and then finished with olives, capers, and basil. ✳ *Cianfotta,* or *cianbotta,* depending on where you are, has come to mean a mélange of vegetables cooked together. The *cianfotta* that I know is a version that is baked, using a combination of autumn vegetables. Gabrio Bini makes a sauce to go with the *cianfotta* that he calls the *contorno* for the *contorno.*

cianfotta alla gabrio bini
gabrio bini's baked vegetables

1 butternut squash, 1½ pounds, peeled, seeded, and cut into 2-by-1-inch pieces

1 pound small red potatoes, parboiled for 10 minutes

1 pound broccoli, cut into florets

1 head cauliflower, 1½ pounds, cut into florets

2 onions, quartered

1 pint cherry tomatoes, stemmed

⅓ cup water

½ cup olive oil

2 teaspoons coarse sea salt

tomato-caper sauce:

1 tin (1 pound) *pelati* (Italian peeled plum tomatoes), undrained, pushed through a sieve

1 rounded tablespoon salt-packed capers, rinsed and finely chopped

2 tablespoons coarsely chopped fresh basil

1. Preheat an oven to 400°F. In a large oval, square, round, or rectangular ceramic or terra-cotta baking dish, arrange the vegetables as you like. Here's how I do it: Stand the squash pieces up around the edge of the dish. Place the potatoes on the bottom. Put the broccoli and cauliflower florets, upright, in between the potatoes and some of the squash. Place the onion quarters in and around the vegetables. Scatter the cherry tomatoes over the top. Splash the water over everything evenly. Drizzle the olive oil over everything. Sprinkle the salt over the top.

2. Bake until the vegetables are soft and the tops of the vegetables are slightly burned, about 1½ hours.

3. While the vegetables are baking, make the tomato-caper sauce: In a bowl, combine the tomato puree, capers, and basil. Stir to mix.

4. Serve the *cianfotta* hot with the sauce.

serves 4 Before pasta became the emblematic food of Italy, there was polenta. Polenta, which is made from milled grains, is derived from the Latin *pulmentum*, meaning "gruel" or "porridge." According to Waverley Root, in *The Food of Italy* (Vintage Books, 1971), it was polenta, a staple of the Etruscans, that fed the conquering Roman army. The polenta of the ancient Romans was probably made with ground barley. Other polentas had been made with millet, sorghum, chestnuts, and spelt, before Christopher Columbus, returning from the Americas, introduced maize to Europe. ※ It's the corn version that springs to mind when we think of polenta today. Polenta is the starch of choice for many in northern Italy, the area once occupied by the Etruscans. While it's no longer a primary source of sustenance, it's sometimes eaten as a first course with a sauce, but more often as a *contorno* to grilled sausages, braised radicchio, *baccalà* (salt cod), with game, and with beef or veal stews. Simply put, it's the mashed potatoes of northern Italy. ※ Here are two recipes, one for a soft polenta, which is an ideal side dish for a saucy entrée, and the other for making a firmer polenta that can be turned into a more elaborate *contorno*. ※ Be prepared to stand by the stove, stirring, for a while. Continuous stirring is essential to achieving a good, smooth polenta.

polenta

polenta morbida / **soft polenta**

6 cups water

1 teaspoon salt

1 cup stone-ground cornmeal

Unsalted butter and grated cheese (optional)

1. In a large pot, bring the water to a rolling boil and add the salt. Slowly add the cornmeal, stirring continuously with a wooden paddle or spoon. If the cornmeal clumps, use a whisk to break up the lumps, then continue stirring with the wooden paddle. As the mixture thickens it will begin to "erupt"; lower the heat to a simmer and continue to stir. When the mixture is thick, smooth, and begins to pull away from the sides of the pot, it's ready, about 40 minutes.

2. Add butter and cheese as desired and serve immediately.

polenta pasticciata / **baked polenta "mess"**

6 cups water

1 teaspoon salt

1¼ cups stone-ground cornmeal

2 tablespoons unsalted butter, melted

¼ cup grated Parmesan cheese

1. In a large pot, bring the water to a rolling boil and add the salt. Slowly add 1 cup of the cornmeal, stirring continuously as for *Polenta Morbida* (preceding recipe). After 15 minutes of cooking time, add the remaining ¼ cup cornmeal and continue cooking as for *Polenta Morbida*. When the polenta is ready, turn it out onto a rimmed baking sheet. Use the wooden paddle or spoon to spread out the polenta to an even ½-inch thickness. Let harden, about 1 hour.

2. Preheat an oven to 350°F. Cut the polenta into 2-inch squares. Use some of the melted butter to grease a baking dish. Make an overlapping layer with half of the polenta squares. Use a pastry brush to brush the polenta with half of the remaining butter. Sprinkle half of the cheese over the layer. Make another layer with the remaining polenta squares. Brush with the remaining butter and sprinkle with the remaining cheese.

3. Bake until the sides are bubbling, about 30 minutes. Turn the oven to broil. Put the dish under the broiler until the top is golden, about 5 minutes. Serve immediately.

serves 6 to 8 *Sformare* means "to pull out of shape." When something is *sformato*, it's shapeless. In culinary terms, a *sformato* is a pudding, sweet or savory, made in a mold—it's hardly shapeless, quite the opposite. ☀ I'm crazy about this chestnut pudding. It's labor-intensive. Big time. Allow yourself an hour to shell this amount of chestnuts. You can take a shortcut and purchase canned chestnut puree, but you'll be missing an essential seasoning element, the bay leaf, which flavors the chestnuts as they cook. *Vale la pena*—"it's worth it"—as the Italians would say. Do it right! Then serve it with game or wild fowl.

sformato di castagne
savory chestnut pudding

1¼ to 1½ pounds chestnuts (allow for some rotten ones)

3 good-quality bay leaves, plus 1 or 2 leaves for garnish (optional)

3 teaspoons salt

1 small onion, finely chopped

2 eggs, lightly beaten

1 cup whole-milk ricotta cheese

1 tablespoon balsamic vinegar

½ teaspoon ground cinnamon

¼ teaspoon freshly ground black pepper

1 tablespoon unsalted butter

1 tablespoon plain dried bread crumbs

1. Fill a large saucepan with water and place over medium heat. Add the chestnuts, 3 bay leaves, and 2 teaspoons of the salt. Bring to a gentle boil and boil the chestnuts for 40 minutes. Drain and let cool to the touch. Use a sharp paring knife to cut the shell away from the chestnut. Peel the skin away, and then cut out any rotten sections. It's okay if not all the nuts come out of their shells in perfect shape. Try to save a few whole ones for garnish.

2. Push the chestnuts through a food mill or ricer held over a bowl. Add the onion, eggs, ricotta, vinegar, the remaining 1 teaspoon salt, the cinnamon, and the pepper. Stir well to combine.

3. Preheat an oven to 350°F. Grease a 4-cup ovenproof bowl with the butter. Add the bread crumbs to the bowl, and tilt the bowl in a circular motion until the surface is evenly coated. Spoon the chestnut mixture into the bowl. Put the bowl in a baking pan and add hot water to the pan to reach halfway up the sides of bowl.

4. Bake until the chestnut mixture starts to pull away from the sides of the bowl, about 45 minutes. Remove from the oven and immediately invert the bowl onto a platter. You may have to coax the pudding a bit by running a knife around the inside edge of the bowl. Garnish with whole chestnuts and perhaps a bay leaf or two.

serves 4 to 6 *Affogata* can be translated as suffocated, smothered, or drowned. For culinary purposes, I think drowned is the most appropriate translation. After all, that's precisely what happens to these turnips in a method of cooking that's very similar to the late-nineteenth-century way of "seething" vegetables. An *affogata* vegetable is simmered in olive oil and water until it's tender—drowning in its liquid—and then sautéed until an intense, pure flavor is achieved. ✳ *Nota bene:* If, when in Italy, you notice *gelato affogato* on a menu, be assured that neither olive oil nor sautéing is involved. It's ice cream drowning in a *caffè espresso*.

rape affogate
"drowned" turnips

1½ **pounds young, small turnips, preferably with their green tops**

¼ **cup olive oil**

2 **tablespoons water**

½ **teaspoon salt**

1 **tablespoon coarsely chopped fresh flat-leaf parsley**

1. Remove the turnip greens. Discard any discolored or rotten leaves. Rinse and set aside. Slice off the root and blossom ends of the turnips. Thoroughly scrub the turnips and cut into ¼-inch dice.

2. In a large skillet or sauté pan over medium-low heat, combine the olive oil, water, and turnip greens. Cook until the greens have just wilted, 3 to 5 minutes. Add the diced turnips and salt, lower the heat, cover, and cook, stirring occasionally, for 15 minutes.

3. Raise the heat, remove the cover, and sauté the vegetables until the liquid has evaporated and the turnips are slightly browned, 5 to 8 minutes. Sprinkle with the parsley and serve immediately.

NOTE: *While the addition of the greens is desirable, they're not essential. Reduce the amount of olive oil by a teaspoon or two if you're not using greens.*

serves 6 My friend Antonia loves squash and ginger. She's from Salerno, where a lot of food is cooked *al tegame*, "in a saucepan," or *in padella*, "in a skillet"—on top of the stove, that is. ✳ This *zucca* dish, an original Antonia creation, was one of the *contorni* gracing her beautiful dining table one evening, midautumn, when I was in Milan gathering information for this book. In my honor, the main course was a selection of *contorni*. A delicious *polpettone*, meat loaf, was offered, offhandedly, to those who absolutely had to have some meat. The occasion reminded me of a rather well-known statement from Thomas Jefferson, who said, "I eat little animal food and that as a condiment for the vegetables."

zucca allo zenzero
squash with fresh ginger

1 tablespoon unsalted butter

1 tablespoon olive oil

3 cloves garlic, sliced paper-thin

1 butternut squash, 2½ pounds, peeled, seeded, and cut into ½-inch dice

2-inch piece fresh ginger, peeled and thinly sliced

¾ cup water

1 teaspoon salt

1. In a large skillet or sauté pan over medium heat, melt the butter in the oil. Sauté the garlic until it turns golden. Add the squash and stir to coat with the oil and butter.

2. Add the ginger, water, and salt and stir to combine. Cook, uncovered, for 30 to 40 minutes. Try not to disturb the squash. Inevitably, two things will occur: some pieces will fall apart and some will get crunchy. When the squash is tender and browned, remove from the heat and serve immediately.

serves 6 to 8 *Zucca*, literally, is pumpkin. The generic *zucca*, the one you find in most Italian markets, looks similar to a Hubbard squash, but in fact has a slightly richer flavor than either the Hubbard or the other kinds of squash or pumpkin sold in American markets. ※ I'm always in favor of using butternut squash when in doubt. The flavor is emphatic, and it's a relatively easy squash with which to work. ※ This gratinéed squash is comfort food supreme. I love it with a whole chicken that's been poached with carrots, onions, celery, and fresh herbs.

zucca gratinata
gratinéed squash

1 butternut squash, 3 pounds, peeled, seeded, and cut into 1-inch cubes

2 white boiling potatoes, about 1 pound total weight

2 eggs, lightly beaten

1 tablespoon all-purpose flour

³/₄ cup whole milk

1 teaspoon salt

topping:

2 tablespoons unsalted butter

2 tablespoons grated Parmesan cheese

2 tablespoons plain dried bread crumbs

¹/₂ teaspoon salt

Pinch of freshly ground black pepper

Fresh sage leaves for garnish (optional)

1. In a large saucepan fitted with a metal steamer, steam the squash until tender, about 15 minutes. Let cool to the touch, then push it through a food mill or ricer held over a large bowl.

2. In a pot with abundant boiling water, cook the potatoes in their jackets until a tester easily passes through them, about 20 minutes. Drain. Peel them as soon as they are cool enough, then push through a ricer or food mill held over the bowl of squash.

3. In another bowl, combine the eggs, flour, milk, and salt. Blend with a small whisk or dinner fork. Add to the squash and stir to thoroughly combine. Transfer to a gratin or shallow baking dish.

4. Preheat an oven to 375°F. Make the topping: In a small bowl, combine the butter, Parmesan, bread crumbs, salt, and pepper. Use your fingers to rub the ingredients together until the mixture is crumbly. Evenly distribute the topping over the squash.

5. Bake until slightly browned and bubbly around the edges, about 30 minutes. Serve immediately. Garnish with sage leaves, if desired.

serves 4 to 6 Do you recall ever seeing a stand of tall, sturdy, small sunflowers growing somewhere in a vegetable garden? Maybe you thought, "What a lovely idea to mix flowers with vegetables." More than likely, however, the roots of those sunflowers were actually the tasty tubers known as Jerusalem artichokes. Jerusalem is a corruption of the Italian word for sunflower, *girasole*, and artichoke refers to the subtle flavor of its tuber. ✳ This recipe treads lightly and doesn't compete with that delicate flavor. Serve it with fish.

topinambur alla panna
jerusalem artichokes cooked in cream

2 tablespoons unsalted butter

1½ pounds Jerusalem artichokes, thinly sliced crosswise

½ teaspoon salt

½ cup heavy cream

½ cup coarsely chopped fresh flat-leaf parsley

1 tablespoon fresh lemon juice

1. In a large skillet or sauté pan over medium heat, melt the butter. Sauté the Jerusalem artichokes until tender, 15 to 20 minutes. Add the salt and cream, lower the heat, and simmer until the cream reduces a bit, 3 or 4 minutes.

2. Remove from the heat and stir in the parsley and lemon juice. Serve immediately.

serves 4 to 6 In the Veneto, many sizes and shapes of radicchio are cultivated. Some of the harvest is eaten raw in a salad, but more often than not, the radicchio is cooked: braised, grilled, or, as in this recipe, baked. The combination of salty pancetta and sweet, nutty Fontina provides just the diversions needed for the moderately bitter radicchio leaf. ✳ This dish is usually made with *radicchio di trevigiano*, or red endive. Its natural tie shape is perfect for this preparation. In our American markets, the tight, round *radicchio di Chioggia* is more readily available. If you use the method that I have devised for this recipe, you'll have a result that's very close to the *radicchio al forno* I enjoy every time I dine at Clemy Viezzer's divine *ristorante*, Il Casteletto, in the Veneto.

radicchio ripieno al forno
baked stuffed radicchio

1 tablespoon unsalted butter

24 medium to large radicchio leaves

¼ pound pancetta or slab bacon, cut into 12 pieces

¼ cup dry white wine

½ teaspoon salt

A few grinds of black pepper

¼ pound Fontina cheese, cut into 12 pieces

1. Preheat an oven to 400°F. Use the butter to grease a large ceramic or terra-cotta baking dish.

2. Make 12 stacks of 2 radicchio leaves each. Place a piece of pancetta in the cavity of each stack. Fold in the sides of the leaves, overlapping them around the pancetta (the finished bundle should resemble a tie), and place, seam side down, in the baking dish. Make 2 rows of 6 bundles each. The first row should be placed along the top half of the width of the dish. The tops of the bundles of the second row will overlap the bottoms of the first row a tiny bit.

3. Sprinkle the wine over the radicchio. Sprinkle on the salt and pepper. Cover the dish with aluminum foil. Bake for 15 minutes.

4. Remove the foil. Raise the oven temperature to 450°F. Place a piece of Fontina on each radicchio bundle. Cook until the cheese melts and is slightly brown, 15 to 20 minutes. Serve immediately.

serves 6 to 8 This oh so *raffinato contorno*, that the Italians love to cook in a ring mold and then, once unmolded, fill with another *contorno*, makes for an extremely elegant presentation. ❋ The recipe for this particular spinach pudding was given to me by my friend Marina Prada Danieli, after I had eaten it at her home. It's a great accompaniment to simple preparations of chicken, beef, or fish.

sformato di spinaci
spinach pudding

4 pounds spinach, thoroughly rinsed and tough stems removed

3 tablespoons unsalted butter

2 tablespoons all-purpose flour

¾ cup milk

½ cup grated Parmesan cheese

1 teaspoon salt

½ teaspoon freshly ground white pepper

3 eggs, lightly beaten

2 tablespoons plain dried bread crumbs

***Funghi Trifolati* (page 93), *Funghi Trippati* (page 90), or sautéed cherry tomatoes; optional**

1. In a large, heavy-bottomed saucepan over medium heat, using the moisture that has remained from rinsing, add the spinach in batches until it all has wilted. If the leaves seem too dry, add ¼ cup water at a time as needed. Remove from the heat, drain, pressing out excess moisture, and let cool. Put through a food mill or finely chop. Place in a large bowl.

2. In a small, nonreactive saucepan over medium heat, melt 2 tablespoons of the butter. Add the flour and cook for 3 minutes, stirring continuously. Add the milk and cook for another 3 minutes, stirring continuously. When the mixture begins to thicken, add the Parmesan, salt, and pepper. Cook, stirring, until the mixture is as thick as sour cream. Add to the spinach and mix well. Add the eggs and stir to combine.

3. Preheat an oven to 375°F. Use the remaining 1 tablespoon butter to grease a 9-inch ring mold. Add the bread crumbs to the mold, and tilt in a circular motion until the surface is evenly coated. Add the spinach mixture to the mold. Put the mold in a baking dish and add hot water to the pan to reach halfway up the sides of the mold.

4. Bake until the spinach starts to pull away from the sides of the mold and the top is slightly browned, at least 1 hour. Remove from the oven and immediately invert the mold onto a platter. You may have to coax the pudding a bit by running a knife around the inside edge of the mold. If desired, choose one of the garnishes to fill the center of the pudding and serve immediately.

serves 6 Here we go again, another vegetable dish named for a style of preparation used for meat. In this case, stewed mushrooms are cooked in the manner of *trippa in umido*, tripe stewed in tomato sauce. If you don't like tripe, don't think about the mushrooms' namesake. ✳ Make these nutty, spicy mushrooms, then serve them with *Polenta Morbida* (page 77) and grilled sausages.

funghi trippati
stewed mushrooms

¼ cup olive oil

3 cloves garlic, smashed, then peeled

2 pounds assorted mushrooms such as cremini, portabella, porcino, and shiitake, brushed clean and thinly sliced

¾ cup tomato puree (not concentrate) diluted with ¼ cup hot water

1 teaspoon dried oregano

1 teaspoon salt

¼ teaspoon ground cayenne

¼ cup grated Parmesan cheese

1. In a large skillet or sauté pan over medium heat, heat the olive oil. Add the garlic and cook, stirring occasionally, for 2 or 3 minutes to flavor the oil.

2. Raise the heat and add the mushrooms. When the mushrooms have released their liquid, lower the heat to medium-low. Add the diluted tomato puree, oregano, salt, and cayenne. Cook until most of the liquid has been reabsorbed—you want a little sauce—about 20 minutes.

3. Transfer to a serving dish and sprinkle with the Parmesan. Serve immediately, or use as a *contorno* with *Sformato di Spinaci* (page 89).

serves 6 This preparation is appropriate whether you want to showcase the flavor of an individual mushroom or of a good mix of mushrooms. In fact, this preparation is so clever in its simple combination of ingredients that it's often the way eggplant and zucchini are fixed. When they are cooked this way, it's called *al funghetto*, "in the mushroom style."

funghi trifolati
truffled mushrooms

2 tablespoons unsalted butter

¼ cup olive oil

3 cloves garlic, smashed, then peeled

2 pounds mushrooms such as cremini, portabella, and porcino, one variety or an assortment, brushed clean and thinly sliced

½ teaspoon salt

A few grinds of black pepper

2 tablespoons coarsely chopped fresh flat-leaf parsley

1. In a large skillet or sauté pan over medium heat, melt the butter in the olive oil. Add the garlic and cook, stirring occasionally, for 2 or 3 minutes to flavor the oil.

2. Raise the heat and add the mushrooms. When the mushrooms have released their liquid, lower the heat to medium-low. Cook until most of the liquid has been reabsorbed—you want a little sauce—and the mushrooms are tender, about 20 minutes.

3. Remove from the heat and remove and discard the garlic. Stir in the salt, pepper, and parsley. Serve immediately, or use as a *contorno* with *Sformato di Spinaci* (page 89).

serves 6 to 8   When I was collecting recipes for this book, this one kept showing up in cookbooks and magazine articles. I was intrigued. Liguria, on Italy's northwest Mediterranean coast, is well known for all sorts of vegetable preparations. The region is sheltered from the northern climate by a barrier of mountains that stands between it and the rest of Italy, affording a long growing season. ❈ Each recipe that I found for *funghi e patate* had its own little twist. For example, you could use fresh basil instead of parsley to season the dish. Or you could chop the seasonings together as with this recipe, which I found in one of my favorite food magazines, *Sale e Pepe*. ❈ This dish can be put together up to 4 hours before baking time.

funghi e patate alla ligure
ligurian-style mushrooms and potatoes

1¼ pounds Yukon gold potatoes, peeled and cut into ⅛-inch-thick slices

¼ cup fresh flat-leaf parsley leaves, finely chopped

2 cloves garlic, minced

1½ pounds porcino or portabella mushrooms, brushed clean, stems finely chopped and caps thinly sliced

½ cup olive oil

1½ teaspoons salt

½ teaspoon freshly ground black pepper

1. In a large saucepan with abundant boiling water, cook the potatoes until nearly tender, about 7 minutes. Drain.

2. In a bowl, combine the parsley, garlic, chopped mushroom stems, ¼ cup of the olive oil, the salt, and the pepper. Stir to combine.

3. Preheat an oven to 425°F. Use 1 tablespoon of the olive oil to grease a ceramic or terra-cotta baking dish. Line the bottom of the dish with the sliced potatoes. Use half of the parsley mixture to cover the potatoes. Layer on the sliced mushrooms. Cover with the remaining parsley mixture. Drizzle the remaining 3 tablespoons olive oil over the top.

4. Cover with aluminum foil and bake for 30 minutes. Remove the foil and bake until a slight crust is visible, about 10 minutes. Serve immediately or at room temperature.

serves 6 Broccoli is cooked more or less this way up and down the Italian peninsula. Sometimes an anchovy and some capers are added; sometimes raisins and pine nuts are added. The thing that makes this recipe *alla romana* is the way that the garlic is treated. It's chopped and remains a part of the finished dish, rather than staying whole throughout the cooking process, then removed just before serving. ✳ If, by chance, you're lucky enough to grow broccoli, or can purchase it from a farm stand, make sure to keep the leaves. Then, add the rinsed leaves to the pan when you add the florets. Not only will they add texture, but another taste dimension as well.

broccoli alla romana
roman-style broccoli

2 pounds broccoli

2 cloves garlic, finely chopped

1/4 cup olive oil

1/4 teaspoon hot pepper flakes

3/4 cup dry white wine

1 teaspoon salt

1. Divide the broccoli into florets, leaving their stems, 1 1/2 to 2 inches long. Peel the stems.

2. In a large saucepan over medium heat, sauté the garlic in the olive oil until pale gold, about 2 minutes. Add the broccoli and stir to thoroughly coat it with the oil. Add the hot pepper flakes, wine, and salt and stir to combine. Cover and cook until the broccoli is tender, not mushy, about 15 minutes. Serve immediately.

serves 6 Just as the *Broccoli alla Romana* (page 95) is a universal preparation, this way of cooking cauliflower is also one used almost everywhere in Italy. As with the broccoli, now that you have the method, you can change the flavoring ingredients as desired. Try adding chopped green olives and anchovies instead of raisins and pine nuts at the same point in the recipe. Because cauliflower is a young cousin to broccoli, recipes for one are usually interchangeable with those for the other. It's all in the family!

cavolfiori con passi e pinoli
cauliflower with raisins and pine nuts

1 head cauliflower, 1½ to 1¾ pounds

1 clove garlic, smashed, then peeled

¼ cup olive oil

4 teaspoons raisins

4 teaspoons pine nuts

2 tablespoons coarsely chopped fresh flat-leaf parsley

½ teaspoon salt, or more to taste

1. Divide the cauliflower into florets. Parboil in boiling water for 5 minutes. Drain.

2. In a large skillet or sauté pan over medium heat, sauté the garlic in the olive oil for 2 minutes to flavor the oil. Add the parboiled cauliflower, raisins, and pine nuts, lower the heat, and cover. Cook, stirring occasionally, until the cauliflower is tender but not mushy, 10 to 15 minutes.

3. Remove from the heat, remove and discard the garlic, and stir in the parsley and salt. Serve immediately.

serves 4 to 8 One of my personal publishing traditions is always to include a recipe from my friends *la famiglia* Bini. The following recipe came from the most unexpected Bini of them all, Genevieve Bini, the French-born wife of my favorite cook, Gabrio Bini. Without diminishing any of Gigi's talents, and there are many, I was happily and completely taken aback when she served me this fruit charred in red wine and fruit *passata* with a selection of cheese one Sunday lunch. ✳ On second thought, why was I so surprised? Gigi is an artist, and artists solve problems, taking you to places where you've never been. What better way to solve the problem of baskets full of fruit—some of it about to go bad—than to create this *contorno* for cheese?

un contorno suo malgrado
a side dish in spite of itself

4 apples, your choice

4 pears, your choice

4 sugar cubes, preferably pure cane sugar

2 cups full-bodied red wine

4 plums, your choice

1½ pounds red or green grapes, stemmed

1. Preheat an oven to 375°F. Dig out a little hole in the blossom end of 2 apples and 2 pears. Put a sugar cube in each opening. Place all the apples and pears in an attractive terra-cotta or ceramic baking dish. Pour the wine over the fruit.

2. Bake, spooning the wine over the fruits every 30 minutes, until the fruits appear soft, but not mushy, and are slightly charred, about 2 hours.

3. While the fruits are baking, prepare the *passata*: In a saucepan or flameproof terra-cotta pot over medium heat, combine the plums and the grapes. Cook until the fruits are soft, 15 to 45 minutes, depending on their ripeness. Remove from the heat and let cool for a few minutes. Use a wooden spoon to push the fruit mixture through a sieve. Return the mixture to the pan over low heat and reduce until the consistency of pancake batter.

4. Pour the fruit *passata* into an attractive serving bowl, and bring it to table with the baked fruit. Serve both fruit preparations warm or at room temperature.

4 *winter* **inverno**

serve 6 I found this recipe in the well-known Italian food magazine *La cucina italiana*. I like it for its simplicity and its familiarity. It reminds me a little of candied carrots. The addition of the sharp turnips and the dry, herby Marsala makes the dish a little less sweet. ☀ Serve this carrot-turnip combo with grilled pork chops.

carote e rape al marsala
carrots and turnips cooked with marsala

2 tablespoons unsalted butter

1 pound carrots, peeled and cut into ⅛-inch-thick slices

1 pound turnips, peeled and cut into ¼-inch dice

¾ cup dry Marsala

1 teaspoon salt

2 tablespoons finely chopped fresh flat-leaf parsley

1. In a large skillet over medium heat, melt the butter. Add the carrots and turnips and stir to coat the vegetables with the butter. Lower the heat and cook for 5 minutes. Add the Marsala and salt and simmer, stirring occasionally, until the wine is absorbed, about 10 minutes.

2. Add the parsley and stir to combine. Transfer to a serving bowl and serve immediately.

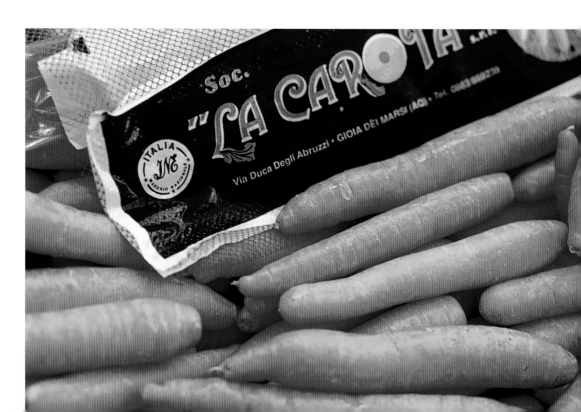

serves 6 Here's a variation of *Carote e Rape al Marsala* (facing page). While honey is a significant part of this ingredient list, so is lemon juice. Sweet and sour is a flavor combination not unknown in the Italian kitchen. It figures, especially, in the foods of southern Italy, where Arab influence is most significant. ✳ So you won't be surprised to learn that this recipe was given to me by my friend Miro Silvera, whose origins are in Syria. Miro told me that these sweet, sour, and fragrant vegetables were made by his grandmother in her kitchen in Aleppo, and again in Italy when the family immigrated to Milan.

carote e sedano-rapa alla nonna silvera
grandma silvera's carrots and celery root

1 celery root, 1 pound, peeled and cut into ½-inch dice

1 pound carrots, peeled and cut into ⅛-inch-thick slices

1 cup water

Juice of 2 lemons

2 tablespoons pure honey

½ teaspoon salt

2 tablespoons coarsely chopped fresh flat-leaf parsley

Extra-virgin olive oil for garnish

Freshly ground black pepper for garnish

1. In a saucepan over medium-low heat, combine the celery root, carrots, water, lemon juice, honey, and salt. Cook, with the cover askew, and stirring occasionally, until the vegetables are tender, about 1 hour.

2. Remove from the heat and stir in the chopped parsley. Transfer to a serving dish. Serve hot or at room temperature. Garnish with a drizzle of olive oil and a few grinds of black pepper.

serves 6 Every once in a while I come across a recipe that strikes me as so interesting that I'm compelled to try it immediately. ✳ About two weeks before I was scheduled to deliver my manuscript, I thought that I had all the recipes necessary to complete this book. Then a friend arrived from Milan with a stack of Italian food magazines for me. The minute that I read the ingredients for this carrot pie, I knew it was a winner. Making a few adjustments to ensure an easy preparation, I cooked this *pasticcio* right away. ✳ Just wait until you taste what happens when the sweet carrots meet the slightly pungent Gorgonzola. You *must* find Gorgonzola dolcelatte, however, as a longer-aged Gorgonzola will be too overpowering. The walnuts contribute texture, and the fresh thyme, fragrance. ✳ This rich *contorno* wants to sit beside a simple roast, pork or lamb. ✳ *Grazie*, Paolo.

pasticcio di carote e gorgonzola
carrot and gorgonzola pie

2 pounds carrots, peeled and cut into ½-inch pieces

1 teaspoon salt, plus salt to taste

2 tablespoons unsalted butter

½ pound Gorgonzola dolcelatte cheese

3 eggs

½ cup plus 1 tablespoon walnuts, coarsely chopped

2 teaspoons fresh thyme leaves, plus 3 or 4 sprigs

¼ teaspoon freshly ground white pepper

1. In a large pot of abundant boiling water, parboil the carrots with the 1 teaspoon salt for 10 minutes. Drain.

2. In a large skillet or sauté pan over medium heat, melt 1 tablespoon of the butter. Sauté the carrots, stirring occasionally, until fork-tender, about 3 minutes. Remove from the heat and transfer to a bowl. Use a potato masher or dinner fork to mash the carrots.

3. Preheat an oven to 350°F. Remove the crust from the Gorgonzola. In a food processor or blender, combine the cheese, eggs, and ½ cup walnuts. Process until perfectly smooth. Use a rubber spatula to incorporate the cheese mixture with the mashed carrots. Stir in the thyme leaves and pepper. Taste for salt and add as needed.

4. Use the remaining 1 tablespoon butter to grease a ceramic or terra-cotta baking dish. Pour in the carrot mixture, and use the spatula to distribute evenly. Place the thyme sprigs on top in a decorative way. Press lightly to anchor them in the surface.

5. Bake until the sides are bubbling and a golden crust has formed, about 30 minutes. Sprinkle with the remaining tablespoon of walnuts and serve immediately.

serves 6 You may ask, "Why is this called sauerkraut and not cabbage?" ☀ Here's the answer. The ingredients in this recipe and the three-hour cooking time combine to create a *finto* (fake) sauerkraut—soft and slightly pickled. ☀ You might find this *contorno* served at a ski lodge in Cortina d'Ampezzo near the Austrian border. Imagine yourself sitting beside a crackling fire, where there's a table set with a platter of assorted, boiled sausages, a basket of dark bread, bowls of pungent mustard and cornichons, and *crauti freschi*. Yes, you are about to feast *all'italiano*, believe it or not!

crauti freschi al bacon
quick sauerkraut with bacon

1 head green cabbage, 2 to 2¼ pounds

¼ pound slab bacon, coarsely chopped

1 tablespoon unsalted butter

½ cup dry white wine

1½ cups vegetable broth or water

Salt and freshly ground black pepper to taste

1. Eliminate the tough outer leaves of the cabbage. Cut the head into quarters through the stem end, and then cut out the core. Use a sharp knife or a mandoline to thinly slice crosswise.

2. In a large skillet or sauté pan over medium heat, cook the bacon and the butter until the bacon renders most of its fat and becomes crisp, 6 or 7 minutes. Add the cabbage and stir with 2 wooden spoons to ensure that all the cabbage is coated with the fat. Cook for 3 minutes. Add the wine and vegetable broth and stir to combine. Lower the heat, cover, and simmer for at least 3 hours, stirring occasionally. The liquid should be almost completely absorbed and the cabbage very soft.

3. Taste for salt and pepper and add as needed. Serve immediately or store in the refrigerator for up to a week. Reheat as needed.

serves 6 The fragrant, licoricey fennel is both sweetened, with the onions, and salted, with the ham and cheese, producing a perfect savory dish. The result is so perfect, in fact, that it proved an ideal companion to roast turkey—and my contribution to a potluck Thanksgiving dinner one year.

finocchi al prosciutto
fennel with ham

4 fennel bulbs

1 tablespoon unsalted butter

2 tablespoons olive oil

1 onion, finely chopped

⅓ pound cooked ham, finely diced

½ teaspoon salt

2 cups chicken or vegetable broth

½ pound Gruyère cheese, finely shredded

1. Remove the hard outside leaves from each fennel bulb. Save a handful of the feathery fronds. Cut each bulb lengthwise into eighths.

2. Preheat an oven to 375°F. In a large, heavy-bottomed saucepan, melt the butter in the olive oil. Add the onion and sauté until translucent, about 3 minutes. Add the fennel, ham, and salt and stir to combine and thoroughly coat the ingredients. Transfer the fennel mixture to a 15-inch gratin dish, and pour in the broth.

3. Bake until the liquid is absorbed, but the dish is not completely dry, 30 to 40 minutes. Remove from the oven and top evenly with the Gruyère. Place the fennel fronds on the cheese in a decorative way. Continue to bake until the cheese has melted and begins to bubble, about 10 minutes. Serve immediately.

serves 6 Leeks, like so many vegetables and herbs that we enjoy today, are prehistoric plants. The Greeks who colonized Rome began serious cultivation of this oversized scallion, which, according to *The Cambridge History of World Food* (Cambridge University Press, 2000), resulted in a longstanding Roman predilection for leeks. The Romans then shared their favorite allium with the rest of Europe. ✳ In this dish, the subtle flavor of leeks is not, as you might imagine, overpowered by the bread crumbs and cheese; it is instead enhanced. However, the gratin should accompany a mild main course.

porri gratinati
gratinéed leeks

6 leeks, roots and green parts removed

3 tablespoons unsalted butter

Scant ½ cup plain dried bread crumbs

¼ pound Emmentaler cheese, shredded

½ teaspoon salt

1. Cut the leeks in half lengthwise, and rinse thoroughly to remove any trace of dirt.

2. In a large pot of abundant, salted simmering water, poach the leeks for 5 minutes. Use tongs to remove them carefully from the water so they stay intact. Let them drain on paper towels.

3. Preheat an oven to 375°F. Use 1 tablespoon of the butter to grease a gratin dish or shallow baking dish. Sprinkle the bottom of the dish with some bread crumbs to cover, then arrange the leeks, cut sides up, on top. Mix the remaining bread crumbs with the cheese and salt. Cover the leeks evenly with the mixture. Melt the remaining 2 tablespoons butter and pour over the tops of the leeks.

4. Bake until the top is browned and apparently crunchy, 30 to 40 minutes. Serve immediately.

serves 6 to 8 The gallery of my friend Antonia Jannone, in the historical center of Milan, is dedicated to architectural drawings and paintings. Antonia's eye is attracted to the precise, and to the quirky. ✳ It was appropriate that I first saw these intense, little tomatoes, lined up in their baking dish looking for all the world like a plan for an all-tomato city, in Antonia's kitchen. ✳ In the early wintertime, after I tasted this incredibly flavorful dish, I broke a steadfast rule about never using fresh tomatoes if they weren't local and vine-ripened. The cherry tomatoes that you find in Italy year-round come from Sicily. The ones we get in the United States come from a variety of places, mostly Central and South America during our cold-weather months. While this dish is well paired with any sort of grilled meat, I love to eat it with a plain omelet.

pomodorini cilegie al forno
baked cherry tomatoes

½ cup extra-virgin olive oil

2 cloves garlic, minced

2 tablespoons finely chopped
    fresh rosemary leaves

1 teaspoon salt

¼ teaspoon freshly ground
    black pepper

50 cherry tomatoes, about
    2 pints, stemmed

2 tablespoons plain dried
    bread crumbs

1. In a bowl, combine the olive oil, garlic, rosemary, salt, and pepper. Stir to mix.

2. Preheat an oven to 350°F. Cut the tomatoes in half crosswise. Line them up, tightly and cut sides up, in a 17-by-11-inch baking pan. Spoon all of the olive oil mixture over the tomatoes. Keep mixing up from the bottom as you do this to ensure that you will have some of every ingredient in each spoonful. Use your fingers to sprinkle the bread crumbs evenly over the tomatoes.

3. Bake the tomatoes until the olive oil mixture is bubbly and golden and the tomatoes begin to look charred, about 1 hour. Serve immediately.

serves 6 to 8 To my mind, *cavolini di Bruxelles*, "little cabbages from Brussels," is a much more descriptive name than Brussels sprouts for this vegetable. It tells the story of these miniature cabbages that grow on a single stalk. The plant was developed, as the name implies, sometime between the thirteenth and seventeenth centuries in Brussels. Each reference book tells a different tale, but in order to tie this vegetable to Italy, thankfully they all agree that it was no doubt a roaming Roman who brought the mother plant, *Brassica olercacea* (the original cabbage, which grew wild on the Mediterranean coast almost twenty-five hundred years ago), to Belgium in the first place.

cavolini di bruxelles al tegame
stewed brussels sprouts

½ pounds Brussels sprouts

1 tablespoon unsalted butter

1 tablespoon olive oil

1 onion, thinly sliced

1 clove garlic, minced

2 slices bacon, coarsely chopped

1 cup chicken or vegetable broth, or water, or as needed

1 teaspoon salt

¼ teaspoon freshly ground black pepper

1 tablespoon coarsely chopped fresh flat-leaf parsley

Sprinkle of freshly grated nutmeg

1. Remove the old and withered leaves from the outside of the Brussels sprouts and score the bottom of each with an X. Plunge the sprouts into salted boiling water and leave there for 2 minutes. Drain and let cool. Quarter each Brussels sprout through the stem end.

2. In a medium saucepan over medium-low heat, melt the butter in the olive oil. Sauté the onion and garlic until the onion is translucent, about 3 minutes. Add the bacon and cook for 1 or 2 minutes until barely crisp.

3. Add the Brussels sprouts, broth, salt, and pepper to the pan and simmer, covered, until the sprouts are tender, about 40 minutes. You may need to add more broth to keep the sprouts from scorching.

4. Add the parsley and nutmeg and stir to combine. Serve immediately.

serves 6 I think that every Italian on the peninsula has cooked a version of this *contorno*. While the choice of greens may vary from chicory to chard, from beet greens to broccoli rabe, it's the greens in combination with potatoes, garlic, and hot pepper that allow the dish to achieve a special texture and zing. ✳ I got this recipe in the Veneto from a dining companion, Paolo De Marzi, one evening while making my usual request for favorite dishes. I was particularly happy to receive it, as I have a weakness for chicory, cooked and raw. Even better, chicory is almost always found on supermarket shelves.

cicoria e patate piccanti
spicy chicory and potatoes

³⁄₄ pound potatoes, preferably Yukon gold

2 pounds chicory, rinsed thoroughly and coarsely chopped

¹⁄₄ cup olive oil

2 cloves garlic, finely chopped

1 teaspoon salt

¹⁄₂ teaspoon hot pepper flakes

1 tablespoon red wine vinegar or fresh lemon juice (optional)

1. In a large pot of abundant boiling water, cook the potatoes in their jackets until a tester easily passes through them, 15 to 20 minutes. Drain, and, when cool enough to handle, peel and cut into ¹⁄₄-inch dice.

2. In a large skillet or sauté pan over medium heat, cook the chicory in the olive oil until it wilts. Add the potatoes, garlic, salt, and hot pepper flakes. Toss to thoroughly combine the ingredients. Cook until the potatoes start to fall apart a bit, 10 to 15 minutes.

3. Add the vinegar or lemon juice to taste, if using. Serve immediately or at room temperature.

serves 8 to 10 This dish is so named because the ingredients used to flavor the beans are the same as those used in a recipe for little birds. Again, vegetarians, don't be put off by this *pres'in giro* (jest), as they're all vegetable.

✳ I'm very, very partial to beans cooked in this style. My reasons are both gustatory and sentimental. *Fagioli con salcicce*—beans, invariably cooked like this, with grilled sausages—was the first dish that I ordered at a trattoria near the Uffizzi Gallery when I arrived in Florence, long ago, to study *le belle arti*. It was an epiphany. Pellicci's Restaurant (the Italian-food reference of my childhood) in Stamford, Connecticut, never had anything resembling this dish on its menu. I was hooked. To this day, these beans with just about anything, but especially with sausages, are a favorite food.

fagioli all'uccelletto
white beans in the style of little birds

1 pound dried white beans such as *cannellini*

¼ cup olive oil

3 cloves garlic, smashed then peeled

10 to 12 fresh sage leaves

4 cups water

1 cup peeled and chopped, fresh or canned plum tomatoes

1 teaspoon salt

1. Put the beans into a large bowl and add 3 times as much water as there are beans. Let soak for at least 8 hours or up to overnight. Drain and rinse the beans.

2. In a large, flameproof, terra-cotta bean pot or a large saucepan over medium heat, warm the olive oil. Add the garlic and sage and cook, stirring occasionally, for 2 or 3 minutes to flavor the oil. Add the drained beans and stir to coat them with the oil. Add the water, lower the heat, and simmer, cover askew, for 45 minutes. Add the tomatoes and simmer until the beans are the desired consistency, about 45 minutes more. The finished beans will hold their shape (for the most part), be tender to the tooth, and be slightly saucy.

3. Add the salt. Serve immediately or at room temperature. The beans can be stored in the refrigerator for up to 4 days and reheated as needed.

serves 6 to 8 *Cipolline* are literally "little onions." However, there is an onion in American markets these days simply called cipollini. They are *cipollina borretana*, a type of yellow-skinned Italian onion that grows small and flat. If you can't find cipollini in your market, substitute small yellow onions—last choice, white pearl onions—for this recipe. ✳ Try these onions on your next holiday table buffet. They're great with roast turkey.

cipolline in agrodolce
sweet-and-sour little onions

2 tablespoons unsalted butter

2 tablespoons olive oil

2 tablespoons sugar

⅓ cup good-quality red wine vinegar

2 pounds cipollini or small yellow onions, peeled and rinsed but not dried

½ teaspoon salt

¼ teaspoon freshly ground black pepper

Chopped fresh mint leaves (optional)

1. In a large saucepan over medium heat, melt the butter in the olive oil. When the butter has melted, add the sugar and stir until it dissolves. Lower the heat, add the vinegar, and simmer until the mixture is the consistency of maple syrup.

2. Add the onions (with a bit of the rinse water still on them), salt, and pepper to the pan. Stir to thoroughly coat with the sauce. Lower the heat, cover, and cook, stirring occasionally, until a tester easily passes through them, about 30 minutes. Serve immediately. Garnish with mint leaves, if desired.

serves 6 This deceptively simple recipe, of a few ingredients, is really an exercise in procedure. ※ In contrast to the easy *Ceci all'Arrabbiata* (page 43), which calls for canned chickpeas, I ask that you make this recipe with the dried ones. There *is* a difference in flavor. The *arrabbiata* preparation includes savory ingredients, slightly diminishing the importance of the chickpea flavor. This puree relies on an essence of chickpea flavor. The results of your labor are well worth the effort. ※ By the time you finish all the steps, the puree will be at room temperature. I like to serve it with steaming hot *Crauti Freschi al Bacon* (page 106).

ceci in pure
chickpea puree

1 pound dried chickpeas

½ cup olive oil

Juice of 1 lemon

1 teaspoon salt

½ teaspoon freshly ground black pepper

2 tablespoons finely chopped fresh flat-leaf parsley

1. Put the chickpeas into a large bowl and add 3 times as much water as there are peas. Let soak for at least overnight or for up to 24 hours.

2. Drain and rinse the peas. In a large saucepan over medium-low heat, combine the peas with twice as much water as there are peas. Cook gently until the chickpeas are almost falling apart, 1 to 1½ hours.

3. Drain the chickpeas. Push through a food mill held over a large bowl.

4. Alternately add 1 tablespoon of the olive oil, then 1 teaspoon of the lemon juice to the pureed chickpeas. Use a wooden spoon to thoroughly beat in the liquid after each addition. Add the salt and pepper.

5. Turn out the puree onto a platter and form a smooth mound. Use the tines of a fork to create circular patterns on the mound. Sprinkle with the parsley and serve.

serves 6 For *Capodanno*, New Year's Eve—or day—the Italians eat coin-shaped food to ensure good fortune and prosperity in the coming year. *Cotechino*, a fat, mild sausage that is boiled and sliced, and lentils are traditional New Year's Eve fare. ❋ Anything goes on New Year's Day, as long as it's round. What could be a more appropriate start to a happy new year than a few stacks of these potato coins, aptly named *monete d'oro*, sitting beside some sliced beef fillet, and either the *Carote e Rape al Marsala* (page 102) or the *Carote e Sedano-Rapa alla Nonna Silvera* (page 103)?

monete d'oro
golden coins

1½ pounds potatoes, preferably Yukon gold

½ cup all-purpose flour, plus more for sprinkling

¼ pound prosciutto, coarsely chopped

1 teaspoon salt

2 cups corn oil

1. In a large pot of abundant boiling water, cook the potatoes in their jackets until a tester easily passes through them, about 20 minutes. Drain. Peel them as soon as they're cool enough to touch, then push them through a ricer or food mill held over a large bowl.

2. Add the flour and the prosciutto, a spoonful at a time, to the potatoes, beating with a wooden spoon after each addition to fully incorporate. Add the salt. You should achieve a dense, smooth dough.

3. Sprinkle some flour on a flat, smooth work surface. Flour a rolling pin. Working with half of the dough at a time, roll it out ¼ inch thick. Use a 2-inch biscuit cutter or a small juice glass to cut out circles. Set them on a platter or baking sheet until all the dough has been cut.

4. Add the oil to a skillet or sauté pan over medium heat, and heat to 365°F. Add the coins, 5 or 6 at a time, to the oil. Move them around and turn them over with a wooden chopstick until they're deep gold and slightly puffed, 2 or 3 minutes. Drain on paper towels.

5. The coins may be kept warm in a 225°F oven until all are cooked and ready to serve. Or they may be made up to 2 or 3 hours ahead and reheated in a 400°F oven. They may lose some of their puffiness, however. Serve piping hot.

serves 6 to 8 You may ask, "Do I really want another risotto recipe? And what's it doing in a book on side dishes?" I answer, "I'm always on the lookout for new twists on old favorite dishes, especially if the recipe has been in a family for years—it adds an air of authenticity." My friend Marina tells me this risotto is not only the way her mother makes it, but it was the way her grandmother made it as well. The family is from Lombardy, the region that gave the world risotto. ❋ Risotto is almost always served as a first course, except when it's the obligatory *contorno* to ossobuco, braised veal shank. It's really the perfect *contorno* to any stew, beef, or chicken. ❋ Consider this risotto instead of mashed potatoes the next time you need something starchy to sop up a sauce.

risotto alla milanese
classic risotto, milan style

4 cups chicken or vegetable broth, or as needed

1 onion, coarsely chopped

2 tablespoons olive oil

1½ cups *carnaroli, vialone nano,* or *arborio* rice

1 cup dry white wine

1 cup milk

¼ teaspoon powdered saffron

¼ cup grated Parmesan cheese

1 tablespoon unsalted butter

Salt

1. In a large saucepan over low heat, bring the broth to a simmer.

2. In a large, heavy-bottomed skillet over medium heat on a burner near the simmering broth, sauté the onion in the olive oil until translucent, about 3 minutes. Add the rice and stir to coat with the oil. Add the white wine and cook, stirring, until the wine is absorbed. Then begin to add the broth, two ladlefuls at a time, cooking and stirring until absorbed before adding more broth. When the rice is al dente, that is, each grain is still hard in the center to the bite, add the milk and saffron and stir until the milk has been absorbed. At this point, the rice should be tender. If it's still too hard, add more broth. The whole cooking time is about 18 minutes.

3. Fold the cheese and butter into the risotto. Taste for salt and add as needed. Serve immediately.

serves 6 In the United States, celery root, it seems, is the darling, the fashionable vegetable of the twenty-first century. The foodies have pureed it, roasted it, braised it, and made it into soups, all of which are then festooned with ingredients that range from foie gras to maple syrup. ✳ Celery root, or celeriac, is a gnarled orb that, when eaten raw, has an earthy flavor something like pungent celery. It calms down a bit when cooked—hence, the jazzy additions. In this recipe, I like the way the cheesy béchamel sauce complements the delicate celery-parsley taste. So, instead of fiddling with this side dish to liven it up, why not let it accompany a spicy main dish?

sedano-rapa alla besciamella
celery root in béchamel sauce

2 celery roots, 1½ to 1¾ pounds total weight, peeled

1 tablespoon unsalted butter

béchamel sauce:

2 tablespoons unsalted butter

2 tablespoons all-purpose flour

1½ cups milk

½ teaspoon salt

¼ teaspoon freshly ground black pepper

⅓ cup grated Parmesan cheese

1. Add the celery roots to a large pot of abundant boiling water, lower the heat to medium, and cook until they are quite soft and a tester easily passes through them, about 1 hour. Drain and let cool to the touch, then cut crosswise into slightly less than ¼-inch-thick slices.

2. While the roots are cooking, make the béchamel sauce: In a small, nonreactive saucepan over medium heat, melt the butter. Add the flour and cook, stirring continuously, for 3 minutes. Gradually pour in the milk while stirring continuously, then cook, stirring, for another 3 minutes. When the mixture is the consistency of pancake batter, add the salt, pepper, and Parmesan. Cook, stirring, until the cheese has melted and combined with the sauce, about 2 minutes. Remove from the heat.

3. Preheat an oven to 375°F. Use the remaining 1 tablespoon butter to grease a gratin dish or shallow baking dish. Arrange half of the celery root slices in an overlapping layer. Cover with half of the béchamel. Make another layer with the slices, and cover with the remaining béchamel.

4. Bake until the sides are bubbling and the top is lightly golden, 30 to 40 minutes. Serve immediately.

index